Plants and Flowers in Tagore's Songs

Plants and Flowers in Tagore's Songs

DEBI PRASAD MUKHOPADHYAY

SAṀSKṚITI

SAṀSKṚITI
C-9020, Vasant Kunj, Ṅew Delhi-110070

ISBN : 978-81-87374-66-4

The Cost of this Publication is partly borne by SYNGENTA FOUNDATION FOR SUSTAINABLE AGRICULTURE

Typeset by Vaibhav Graphics, New Delhi
Printed at Mahalaxmi Printers, New Delhi
Published by M. Sengupta for Saṁskṛiti, New Delhi

To

Sheela, My Wife

and

Rahul, My Grandson

CONTENTS

Acknowledgements xi

Foreword xiii

Overview xv

Remarks about the Book xvii

Preface xix

Introduction xxiii

Plants and Flowers in Science and Lyrics xxxi

Chapters

1. Ashath-Ashathwa-Ashwath *(Pipal 'Bo'-tree)* 1
2. Ashok, Banjul *(Asoka tree)* 3
3. Am, Amra, Amua, Sahakar *(Mango)* 7
4. Amlokee, Amloki *(Amla, Emblic myrobalan)* 10
5. Amrha *(Hog-plum)* 12
6. Kachu *(Arum)* 13
7. Kadamba, Kadam, Neepa *(Kadam)* 14
8. Kanakchanpa *(Maple twist)* 18
9. Karabee *(Oleander, Rose bay)* 20
10. Kanchan *(Mountain ebony)* 22
11. Kaminee *(Chinese box, Orange jessamine)* 25
12. Kash *(Thatch grass)* 27
13. Kantalata *(Thorny weeds)* 29
14. Kusum *(i) Lac tree, ii) Safflower iii) Flower* 31
15. Krishnakali, Sandhyaphul, Sandhyakali, Sandhyamalatee *(Four O' Clock plant)* 35
16. Krishnachurha (Radhachurha) *(Peacock flower, Barbados pride)* 37
17. Keya, Ketokee *(Screwpine)* 39
18. Golakchanpa *(Pagoda tree)* 42
19. Golap *(Rose)* 44
20. Chandan *(Sandalwood tree)* 47

21. Chanpa, Champak, Champa *(Golden champa)* 49

22. Jaba *(China rose)* 53

23. Jam, Jambu *(Indian black berry, Java plum)* 55

24. Jnui Jateeya phul *(Jasmines)* 57

25. Kunda *(Kund-jasmine)* 59

26. Chameli, Jati *(Spanish jasmine)* 61

27. Joothee, Junthi, Jnui *(Jnui-jasmine)* 64

28. Banmallika *(Wild jasmine)* 68

29. Bela, Beli, Bel, Ballika *(Arabian jasmine)* 70

30. Mallika, Malli *(Malli-jasmine)* 72

31. Malatee, Malateelata (Jasmine and others)
(i) Malti (Jasmine) (ii) Malatilata (Aganosma) 74

32. Jhau *(Casuarina, She-oak)* 78

33. Jhumkolata *(Passion flower)* 80

34. Tamal, Tamalee *(Egg tree)* 82

35. Tal, Talee *(Palmyra palm)* 85

36. Doorba *(Doob grass, Bermuda grass)* 88

37. Dolonchanpa *(Ginger lily, Butterfly lily)* 92

38. Dhan, Aush *(Rice)* 93

39. Dhutro *(Thorn apple)* 96

40. Nagkeshar *(Iron-wood tree)* 98

41. Narikel *(Coconut tree)* 100

42. Neelshatadal, Neelpadma, Neelambuj *(Blue lotus)* 102

43. Padma, Shatadal, Nalinee, Kamal *(Lotus)* 104

44. Palash, Kimshuk *(Parrot tree, Flame of the forest)* 110

45. Parijat *(Holy tree)* 113

46. Parul *(Trumpet flower)* 116

47. Piyal *(Cuddapah almond)* 118

48. Bakul *(Indian medlar, Spanish cherry)* 121

49. Bot *(Banyan tree)* 127

50. Banaphul Banalata *(Wild flowers and Wild climbers)* 130

51. Bans, Benu *(Bamboo)* 133

52. Madhuk, Mohua *(Mohua tree, Indian butter tree)* 136
53. Madhabee, Madhabika *(Madhabi)* 138
54. Rangan *(Ixora)* 141
55. Rajaneegandha *(Tuberose)* 143
56. Labangalata *(Luvunga)* 145
57. Shamee *(Sami)* 147
58. Shara *(Pin-reed grass)* 148
59. Shal *(Sal)* 149
60. Shimul *(Silk cotton tree)* 152
61. Shireesh *(Siris, Frywood tree Woman's tongue tree)* 154
62. Shephali, Shiuli, Shephalika *(Night jasmine)* 157
63. Shyaola, Shaibals *(Algae)* 161
64. Sojne *(Drumstick)* 163
65. Sorshe *(Sarson)* 165
66. Sneuti *(Himalayan musk rose)* 167
67. Hena *(Henna, Egyptian privet, Tree mignonette)* 169

Plants and flowers *(named by Tagore)* 171
Glossary of Botanical and Horticultural terms 198
Bibliography 205
Flowering calendar of plants and flowers in the text 209
Numerical frequency of plants and flowers in lyrics 229
Index of songs (List of songs in text) 232
Index of English names 251
List of colour Photographs 259

ACKNOWLEDGEMENTS

- Smt. Suchitra Mitra, Kolkata
- Prof. Bharati Mukherjee, Kolkata
- Prof. Rathindra Narayan Basu, Kolkata
- Prof. Tarun Kumar Bose, Kolkata
- Dr. Partha Ranjan Dasgupta, Kolkata
- Dr. Bimal Chowdhury, Kolkata
- Dr. Rathin Kumar Chakraverty, Kolkata
- Dr Debasish Mukherjee, Palampur, Himachal Pradesh
- Shri Subhas Guha Niyogi, Kolkata
- Shri Nilanjan Mukherjee, Shibpur, Howrah
- Smt. Madhusree Mukherjee, Kolkata

FOREWORD

PROF. BHARATI MUKHERJEE
Former Vice-Chancellor,
Rabindra Bharati, University Kolkata

When Tagore was a child he had to sit alone for hours in the portico of Jorasanko Thakurbari within the lakshman rekha drawn by the servant. This solitary confinement offered a unique opportunity to child Rabi to come close to Nature and to face the Nature with all her serenity, to probe into her wonders and to get identified with her beauty. This realization has been reflected in Gurudeva's lifelong literary creations. Plants and flowers are the most beautiful and living manifestation of Nature. This perhaps enthused the poet to mention multifarious indigenous as well as foreign plants and flowers in his most lustrous creations – his lyrics. In many instances the poet has given indigenous names to those of foreign origin. All these focus the poet's intimate and hearty relationship with the world of plants and flowers and depth of his knowledge in plant science.

It is really heartening that Dr Debi Prasad Mukhopadhyay who for decades is a floriculturist by profession, is indeed a Rabindraite by vision. In the well written book 'Plants and Flowers in Tagore's melody' Dr. Mukhopadhyay has collected all the names of Plants and flowers as used by the poet in his 482 songs mentioned in unabridged edition of the Gitabitan. The beauty and speciality of the work, however, lie elsewhere. The author has not only been captured by the melody in plants and flowers, but with a scientist's bent a short description of each of them, its use and values in public life, available literary and mythological background have been incorporated. To meet botanical and horticultural curiosities, scientific names of the plants and flowers together with their families and other necessary information have also been presented in simple language. A number of coloured photographs of different plants and flowers have made the work more attractive.

I am confident that for people to whom Rabindranath is the pathfinder in the life's uphill journey and particularly for Rabindra – researchers this book will be accepted as an invaluable addition to unveil a new dimension of multifaceted genius of the poet which remained hitherto unknown. I would like to convey my heartiest congratulation to the author.

28.5.2009

OVERVIEW

RATHINDRA NARAYAN BASU
Former Vice-Chancellor
Calcutta University, Kolkata

I have read the book of Dr. Debi Prasad Mukhopadhyay's RABINDRASANGEETE UDBHID O PHUL in Bengali. This volume has been rendered in English. All plants and flowers that have been mentioned in Tagore's entire compilation of songs have been alphabetically depicted as in the order of the GITABITAN – the language used being exceptionally easy flowing and readily comprehensible. This makes the book an enjoyable reading material.

It is an undeniable truth that no mention of plants or flowers in poetry, literature, songs or arts can be done with any degree of authenticity without a true introduction whose veracity cannot be denied. The great poet's compositions have amazed readers all over the world, by the manner in which he has put all these to use ever so adroitly; further, the depth of his knowledge of the characteristics of the world of plants and flowers and every painstaking detail never fails to astound even experts in the subject.

The unique subject matter of this book and the manner in which it has been put to use certainly deserves accolades. What is most praisewothy is, instead of delving into the depths of plant life, their weighty scientific names, detailed background, characteristics and use for public welfare etc., an effort has been made to make this easily accessible to average readers in every possible way. Alongside there are also references to ancient poetry, there too references to plant life have been depicted.

All the plants that have been referred to in this book are not unknown in the various regions of India. Hence this book will be treasured by botanists, those specializing in flowers, people all over India and the world who love Tagore and of course who love flowers – in short, the book will be greatly appreciated by large sects of society and humanity in general.

This endeavour of the author should be regarded as a tribute to the memory of one of the greatest poets and lyricists of the world by a distinguished expert on plants and flowers having a poetic mind. I felicitate and thank the writer for this beautiful and unique book and also for its simple style of presentation.

October 2009

REMARKS ABOUT THE BOOK

Suchitra Mitra
51D Gariahat Road
Flat No. 1006
Kolkata 700 019
Tel.No. 2461-8897

Dr. Debi Prasad Mukhopadhyay, a floriculturist by profession is a great admirer of Tagore's work. Rabindrasangeet (Tagore songs) is a passion with him. This inherent love for Tagore songs led him to publish a unique Bengali book - *'Rabindrasangeete Udbhid O Phul'* in 1999 with a short prologue given by me. Its Hindi version came out in 2002. It is a matter of great satisfaction that he continues the job till yet and completes its English version entitled, *'Plants and Flowers in Tagore's Songs'* in a somewhat modified form with more additions and incorporations therein with a view to spreading the theme of his work to a larger section of Tagore lovers all over the world. I have my blessing to such an attempt by the author and wish him every success in his venture. I have no doubt that this book will be appreciated by all who love Tagore and his great creative skill of diverse kinds.

02.09.2009
Kolkata

PREFACE

I have never practised singing in tune, neither have I taken any musical lessons — rather it is something I hold very close to my heart. I consider myself a devoted listener. It follows quite naturally that songs of Tagore are an abiding passion, which I listen to with rapt attention not for the song itself but to understand the inner theme and philosophy contained in such compositions. After listening to many renowned exponents of music, it seems to me that merely singing in scale or according to notations does not truly bring to life the beauty of Tagore songs—words, tune, expression and form, a merging of all four results in the true beauty finding expression in conveying the *bhava* (essence) and evoking the *rasa* (sentiment expressed). This unity remains impossible without a true understanding of the facts and subject matter. It has further occurred to me a number of times that the singer does not truly have a grasp of what the song is all about. As a lover of flowers and as someone who has studied them intensively, I have naturally spent a lot of time thinking about them and a point I have noted that whenever there has been a reference to flowers in songs, Rabindranath Tagore referred to innumerable flowers – foreign and domestic—in his songs. It suddenly sprang to my mind – how many songs exactly did Tagore compose and in them how many times have particular flowers been mentioned. Later, this thought also came to mind – if a compilation and inherent connection can be made of the flowers used in songs and their scientific background, both might stand to gain. The idea of this merging of songs of Tagore and a scientific study of plants and flowers came to me almost 10 years ago. Immediately, I shared my thoughts and idea with the extremely-talented singer and a well-wisher of mine—Smt. Swapna Ghosal.

She appreciated the subject matter I had chosen. In the composition of this book, I have been greatly encouraged by her and she has practically helped by lending me a copy of her book Akhanda Gitabitan (Unabridged version of the Gitabitan). I am greatly indebted to her for her interest, enthusiasm and encouragement.

Smt. Sheela Mukherjee, my wife and Shri Nilanjan Mukherjee, my son, supported me immensely during the preparation of the manuscript. It would not have been possible for me to complete this job but for their active cooperation. It was due to the keen interest and untiring efforts of my wife that the original Bengali version of the book could be published.

Smt. Krishna Mukherjee and Shri Malay Mukherjee are proficient in Tagore literature. Their well-thought-out comments on the manuscript prior to publication have been of invaluable help to me. I am grateful to them.

Besides those I have mentioned, I express my heartfelt gratitude to all others who have helped me by lending books, sketching pictures and in many other ways. In this context, the name of Dr. Sharmistha Roy of Baulmon Prakashan, Kolkata, must be mentioned. Her earnestness and zeal have helped immeasurably in the publication of the Bengali version of the book – *Rabindrasangeete Udbhid O Phul* in January, 1999. Later, after a lot of persuation, the Hindi version of this book *Rabindrasangeetme Prayukt Udbhid Aur Phul* could also be published from her publishing house in April 2002. I remember her efforts and suggestions with gratitude. I am equally indebted to Shri Madhumoy Sengupta, Sanskriti, New Delhi, for kindly agreeing and taking ample initiative to publish this modified English version. Among others who have helped are Shri Gyanranjan Santra, (ex-Curator, Eden Gardens, Kolkata), Shri Arabinda Ghosh, (ex-Garden Superintendent, Raj Bhavan Gardens, Kolkata), Dr. Dulal Chandra Pal (ex-Botanist, Indian Botanic Garden, Howrah) and Shri Prasanta Kumar Maity, Gadmaina, East Midnapur, West Bengal — my thanks to all of them. It was, Dr. Partha Ranjan Dasgupta, a renowned figure in the field of agriculture and horticulture, who, out of his own initiative, came to my help by negotiating with the publisher of Delhi for publishing this volume. I am thankful to him for this exemplary attitude in conveying his love and appreciation of the theme of my work. It is also my pleasure to thank Shri Mrityunjay Bhattacharjee, proprietor, Global Communications, Shibpur, Howrah, for video entry of the manuscript and CD-writing. His devotion to his job for a perfect display of materials indeed is praiseworthy. Finally, I gratefully acknowledge the assistance of all those involved in the preparation of this book.

In course of my long working life and close association with flowering and ornamental plants in gardens for more than three decades, I spent most of the time researching and studying plants and flowers and published nearly10 books and over 50 scientific papers and articles in various scientific magazines and journals. Besides, writing on this different subject matter has given me great pleasure and satisfaction because of the theme, which links subjects like floriculture and Tagore's song compositions. However, I feel that the most adventurous part of this work is my humble and, simultaneously, a very bold endeavour to venture on rendition in English of almost all relevant extracts from the lyrics, poems and literary writings of Tagore. In my attempt, I have tried to be faithful to the theme expressed by the poet and as understood by me. However, I owe my readers an apology for any shortcomings in my attempt. In this regard, I was encouraged by some observations of Anna Racova, a renowned translator, on the job of translation, which I quote: "I have repeatedly heard it said that a translation is like a woman: when it is beautiful, it is not faithful, and the other way round, when it is faithful, it is not beautiful".

My effort will be amply rewarded if this book, in somewhat different form, with more additions and corrections to the earlier Bengali text, helps in understanding and identifying plants and flowers used in Tagore songs and reaches the flower lovers, exponents of Tagore songs, admirers of Tagore's literary and artistic creations, researchers and scientists dealing with plants and flowers.

Debi Prasad Mukhopadhyay

December, 2009
Kolkata

INTRODUCTION

Flowers are precious gifts of nature lending colour, form and fragrance to their bouquet of delights. This is the reason why a lyricist or poet uses flowers in songs and verses to give expressions to emotions through beautiful word pictures. Readers of literature are so accustomed to such use that they often fail to realize the effort involved in employing flowers in just the right way to represent the image in a lyricist's mind. A mustard field sets the blue horizon on fire with its massive floral blooms (*Neel digante oi phuler agun laglo, "Prakriti,"* 202), we hear in a song of Tagore. The poet knows well that mustard plants bloom all of a sudden, filling the fields with brilliant yellow flowers (*Sorshe kshete phul hoye tai jaglo*). The wind sends the flames dancing over the fields, he continues, and in our mind's eye we see yellow waves rippling into the distance [*Sorshe kshete dheu hoye tai jaglo*). It is a glorious invocation of spring-time's heady joys. It is worthwhile to mention here that without adequate knowledge of botanical character, morphology and behaviour of mustard crop under cultivated condition, such perfect composition was not possible. Tagore was an ardent lover of nature and a passionate observer to natural changes in different seasons of the year. No other analogy from the entire plant population could have served his purpose so well.

Our principal lyricist, whose works reside among the world's immortal treasures, employed 67 types of plants and flowers in his nearly 2500 songs, invoking them about 700 times. In his poems, Tagore mentioned 108 kinds of plants. Most of these are familiar to us and contain not only the beautiful or fragrant but also the most ordinary like the Arum (Kachu). "*I hide silently in the arum bush*". ('*Chup kore ei kachuboney lukiye thaki*', Balmeeki Prateeva, scene IV), a fearful dacoit relates. Besides this, we find *Sojne* (Drumstick), *Sorshey* (Sarson/ mustard), *Banamallika* (Wild jasmine), *Tal* (Palmyra palm), many kinds of grasses and other species that thrive uncared for in villages. The poet uses them deftly, lovingly revealing a heart that values every creation of nature, however trifling. Indeed, the small and the insignificant often seems dearer to him than the spectacular. There is also mention of a number of exotic flowers, some of which have been adopted with their native names, others have been lovingly re-named in his own inimitable style to fit into the Indian background. Of course, he did not make use of them in his songs, but there is mention of them in his poetry, e.g. *Madhumanjaree* (Rangoon creeper), *Neelmonilata* (Purple wreath), *Himjhuri* (Indian cork tree), *Sonajhuri* (Australian wattle), *Tarajhara* (Clematis), *Souravee* (Sweet pea), etc. He also named some local flowers like the *Bonpulak* (White paveta), meaning Joy of forest, *Basantee* (bird's eye bush), etc. It is to be kept in mind that it is the common and known flowers that find repeated mention in his songs. *Padma* (Lotus) under a lot of synonyms has been mentioned 101 times {not counting the *Neelpadma* [Blue lotus}, *Bokul* (Indian medlar) 73 times, *Kusum* 46 times, *Malatee* (Malti) 41 times, *Shephali* (Night jasmine) 32 times, *madhabee* (Madhabi) 31 times, *Bans* (Bamboo) 30 times, *Joothee* (Jasmine) and *Kadamba* (Kadam) 28 times, Chanpa (Golden champa) and Grasses including *Doorba* (Doob grass) 25 times, *Palash* (Parrot tree) 23 times, *Ashok* (asoka) 22 times, *Am* (Mango) and *Dhan* (Rice) 21 times and so on.

It is amazing how such a bewildering variety of flowers can find such appropriate and accurate usage in his songs. Songs typifying different stages and emotions find just the precise flower that does it justice. In order to spread a web of magic across the earth the moon needed the help of *Parijat* (Holy tree), the neglected wild *Kachu* (Arum) gave shelter to the cowardly dacoit, covering beneath a facade of bravado. The poet's phenomenal genius had definitely helped him in such living depictions, but the intense love he had for nature and his mastery over the language made this easily viable. He took lessons from nature in a scientific frame of mind. Tagore undertook a comprehensive study of trees, flowers and fruits — he studied at length details of their outward beauty, fragrance, procreation etc. Hence there is an easy flow of comparisons, which become typically associated with certain flowers. In a world pulsating with life, the poet has carved his own niche, the poet's mind has thrilled with the sweet fragrance of the flowers, but then he has also portrayed the pain of an untouchable woman through the imagery of flowers (The flower kissed gracefully the earth to have found its place in the dust. The dust cleansed its heart to cast into purity). "Allow me to forget that I am born in the dust, there is no dust inside me" (Janmo niyechhi dhulitey/daya kore dao bhulitey/nai dhuli mor antarey), he writes, comparing a flower with a fallen woman.

The abiding love that the poet had for flowers must have had its roots in his childhood. But, from the time he set up the centre of learning, Visva-Bharati, all by himself – a number of examples of his love for flowers become highlighted. Shri Jogendrakumar Chattopadhyay writes: 'Santiniketan is like a beautifully nurtured garden; this garden is the home of a variety of fruit trees and flowers ... ("Visva-*Bharatir Ankur,*" *Prabasee,* January 30, 1939). Shri Debiprasanna Chattopadhyay writes : "In 1901, Gurudev Rabindranath Tagore, accompanied by his wife and sons, left for Santiniketan. He planted his favourite trees – mango, sal, amla, and others – as well as ornamental plants, putting his botanical knowledge to practical use. Special mention of these may be found in his lyrics, poems and other literary works. The naming of avenues such as *Amra-kunja* (Mango grove), *Shal beethi* (Sal avenue), *Bokul beethi* (avenue of Indian medlar), Amlaki-bon (Amla groves), *Madhabee kunja* (Madhabi bower), etc., bears testimony to his love for plants and flowers.

Tagore's daughter-in-law Pratima Devi has portrayed an intimate picture of the love the poet had for flowers. She writes, "The trees in Uttarayan were a particular favourite of his. How the *Shimul* (Silk cotton tree) in front of Konark would grow, what fertilizers the tree would need, which climber upon it would enhance its beauty ... he always used to think. To the rear of Konark he earmarked a site for planting *Kontikari* (yellow-berried night shade) and other spiny and thorny plants ... The poet was also responsible for a number of flowers being renamed. If someone chanced upon some beautiful flowers with a bewitching fragrance while walking along the banks of the Kopai, he would request it to be brought and have it planted in Santiniketan. Probably it was a wild flower like this, which was brought in from the Kopai riverside and he named it *'Bonpulak',* meaning joy of the forest. That tree was planted in front of the house at Udayan and still remains there. {"Rabindranath's *Pushpapreeti*" (Tagore's love for flowers), *Prabasee* January 1939}. (Translated).

From all these writings we find a picture of Tagore that was not of an indulgent poet who lived in an ivory tower... we get the distinct impression of a man who enjoyed the fragrance of flowers and savoured their beauty. This presents the picture of a person who would carefully oversee what kind of tree was to be planted at which spot, how it would be carefully nurtured and which climber would further enhance its beauty. It is small wonder, therefore, that he was able to write so spontaneously, "There swings the malati climber on the piyal tree (cuddapah almond)/the east wind caressing it gently" *("Oi malateelata doley piyal tarur koley/pubhaoatey")*, wrote Tagore in a song set during monsoon rains, a time of romance. The poet was delighted at the sight and took every care so that these two could grow and blossom in due course without any complications. But his imagination and artistic views on plants and flowers never stopped his eagerness to know them intimately. He took a very scientific approach to know about the form and structure of these plants. It is almost impossible to find any equal to the comparisons he used with flowers as similes or the depth of his artistic renditions. An unending thirst for knowledge led him to move towards the world of flowers and become more intimately acquainted with them. The poet was not merely satisfied with finding names of flowers that rhymed with his compositions... he lovingly searched to find out more about that particular flower, what its nature was truly like. In a letter written to Indira Devi Chowdhurani he writes: "Flowers bloom on branches – those are their shelter. But men find a place for them in their hearts by giving them special names. ... In this long list of names there are repeated references of *Joothee, Jati, Seunti.* Feeling quite happy if the flowers happen to rhyme, but there is no enthusiasm to ask what flower is known as *Jati* or *Seunti.* After a lot of queries, I have managed to find out that *Chameli* is also known as jati but the real identity of seunti remains unknown till yet in spite of vigorous efforts." (Letter No. 42, Pathey O Pather Prantey, Rabindranath Tagore). (Translated)

The indelible and undeniable proof of love Tagore had for flowers and the extreme practicality that kept him firmly grounded is clearly apparent in sending his son, Rathindranath, to the United States to undertake a rigorous course in agriculture. On his father's instructions Rathindranath started work on various developmental aspects in Santiniketan– Sriniketan complex in 1921–22. Owing to the unstinting and tireless efforts of Rathindranath and his wife Pratima Devi, the entire area was transformed into a peaceful habitat of natural vegetation away from the bustle of city life and similar to *ashramas* of ancient *rishis* of India — a sylvian retreat famed for its gardens and groves. Santiniketan literally means an abode of peace. In order to truly appreciate this, one will have to keep in mind the picture of the region as it was prior to these changes ...dry, barren and practically without any vegetation. Recollecting the time when Pramathanath Bishi, an eminent litterateur of Bengal and a student in Santiniketan between the years 1910-16, writes, "In those days (1910-16) there were virtually no flowers in Santiniketan. I remember walking almost six to seven miles just to get some flowers of *Palash* (Parrot tree),". (*Desh,* Special edition 1965 .... Pramathanath Bishi.) (Translated)

The poet was certainly not content with tree plantation only. Throughout his extremely busy life he kept a careful watch that the plants were being attended to and care was being taken for their maintenance. Even in his old age when he was unwell and bed-ridden most of the time writhing in pain, he was greatly concerned about the garden. On April 27, 1940, he wrote to Shri Alu Roy (Sacchidananda Roy), a devoted worker of Santiniketan, "Pay particular attention to the garden. Some two to three *Chameli* (Spanish jasmine) bushes have to be made close to each other and make its name worthwhile. I love big trees but not too near the house. Remember the *Sojne* tree (drumstick).. it blossoms during winter months, but does not take much time to grow. The *Mahaneem* (Perisian lilac), *Shimul* (Silk cotton tree) easily take to the soil there. A fence made of palte *Madar* (Indian coral tree) has both flowers and thorns as well and the *Bonjuin* (Wild pretty jasmine) also makes a good fence. Cows do not chew on *Raktakarabee* (red oleander), yet the flowers are beautiful. Sada *karabee* (white oleander) and *Lal karabee* (Red oleander) will look good alongside each other. I like the scent of lemon flowers, make sure you have some." — Rani Chanda, Gurudeva, p.93, 1962 (Translated). In his memoirs Jeebansmriti the poet says, "The

Chalta tree (Elephant apple) has in it the beauty of flowers. I am fond of *Shireesh* (Siris), *Jarul* (Queen crape myrtle), *Golapjam* (Rose apple) because of their flowers. Throughout the summer months they require watering. After making appropriate arrangements the *Kurchi* (Easter tree) and *Kanchan* (Mountain ebony) may be planted alternately. No harm in planting one or two *Gandharaj* (Gardenia). What I am not fond of are *Kadamba* (Kadam) and *Chhatim* (Devil's tree). Try and find out why in that place of mine, the *shireesh* (siris) is not growing properly." (Prabhat Kumar Mukhopadhyay, Rabindra jeebanee, p.350, 1964) (Translated).

But this personal likes or dislikes of his did not find any reflection in his poetry or songs. What is amazing is that the *Kadamba* (Kadam) has been mentioned about 28 times in his songs. Just like the other flowers, this one too has certain particular associations. The first blossom of *Kadam* appears in a cloudy overcast day, they appear suddenly and fade away unobtrusively. The poet has made full use of this characteristics of the flower in his memorable song, "*Badala diner prathama kadama phul .... aj eney diley hoyto dibey na kal/rikto hobey je tomar phuler dal*" - The Rainy seasons' first kadamba flower may not be there beyond today/your boughs will wither to weary dryness). The manner in which he has put the flowers to other uses is also remarkable. The *chhatim* (Devil's tree) is the very heart and hub of Santiniketan.

In this book the reader will find, according to their appearance in *Gitabitan*, a complete pictorial list of each and every plant and flower, mentioned and used by Tagore in particular songs along with their brief introduction. Instead of going into high-sounding scientific names and explanations, an attempt has been made to explain the typical characteristic of each flower or plant in an easy manner. Translation of relevant parts of Tagore's songs, poems and literature in English has also been made in a simple way with a view to conveying their essence, sentiments and philosophy as I have conceived. It is my earnest hope that this volume will help readers to pursue the objective of knowing names of all the flowers the poet has used in his songs and gain a better understanding of them, and also to appreciate Tagore's masterly use of his knowledge in horticulture and gardening in lyrics, poems and other writings.

PLANTS AND FLOWERS IN SCIENCE AND LYRICS

The creators of poetry and literature – poets and litterateur— are natural worshippers of beauty. Of all beautiful elements on this earth, flowers hold the highest place – they are an astounding creation of nature. Hence there has been an abiding interest in the beauty of flowers among poets and others involved in the creation of literature. From ancient times an eagerness has found expression through poetry and literature in the appreciation of flower gardens, parks, flowering trees and flowers in general. A worthwhile comparison to all that is tender, delicate and beautiful can be done only by bringing in flowers. It is often said 'as beautiful as a flower'. It seems highly unlikely that there is anything ugly that can be compared to a flower of quality. A proper and seemly comparison in literature and poetry to plants and flowers is only possible when there is a practical knowledge and application of these matters. It is necessary to know their identities, characters and behaviour for perfect literary expression.

In this book, the use of *Shamee-briksha* (Sami tree) as cited in lyrics, clearly indicates that the poet was well versed about plant characters. Or else, how could he say "*Shamee shakhar baksha hotey jemon jwaley agni*"— (Like the fire flame generated from the bosom of sami branches). *(Chandalika*, scene III). Without a thorough knowledge of this plant such a unique comparison was improbable. There are a number of plants in this book that have been alluded to, not because of the beauty of their flowers but because of the qualities they possess and their characteristics, e.g. the *Aswath* (Pipal), *Am* (Mango), *Amloki* (Amla), *Kachu* (Arum), *Jhau* (Casuarina), *Tal* (palmyra palm), *Narikel* (Coconut), *Shara* (Pin-reed grass), *Shyaola* (algae), etc. Thus the poet did not restrict himself only to beautiful flowers but felt equal enthusiasm to know every detail of a plant in nature. He undertook a lot of efforts to find out correct identities of plants like *Jati/Chameli* (Spanish jasmine) and *Sneuti* (Musk rose) as later narrated by him. I recollect a particular incident. Quite a few years back when I was in service one day an artist was sent to Indian Botanic Garden by Satyajit Ray, the universally acclaimed film director, artist and writer, to collect information on a specific plant – *Parul* (Trumpet flower)— after studying its live specimen. In the course of discussion with him it was revealed that the director needed it to do justice to its reference in one of his films under production. This incident clearly justifies the necessity of details of live plants for portraying their true characters in art and literature leaving no scope for undue imagination. So the study of plants is not the prerogative of scientists only; it is perfectly natural for artists, poets and litterateurs to feel alike on the specific plants and flowers they mention in their works.

In the songs of Tagore, *Phul* and *Kusum* (both indicating flower), have been used in abundance without referring to any particular flower, talking of flowers in general and speaking of their natural characteristics. Some such mentions are:

i) "*Phul baley dhanya ami, dhanya ami matir porey*" {I am proud to be associated with soil, says the flower) {Prem and Chandalika}.

ii) "*Phuler gandhe chamak legey uthechhe mon metey (My mind dances with the magic effect of fragrant flowers)* —From the original song '*Akash bhara surya tara*" in Prakriti.

Hence a scientific explanation of some of the floral features would not be inappropriate here.

To scientists flowers are usually odorous, unicoloured or multi-coloured modified shoots to help in bringing about pollination and fertilization in plants. They are later converted to fruits and from the seeds that are thus contained, new plants spring to life. In other words, modifications of stems and leaves give birth to flowers. The arrangement of such flowers in a particular fashion on a rachis (inflorescence axis) is known as inflorescence.

Different flowers have different hues. Flowers of some ornamental plants are conspicuous by their colour, viz. the *beli* (Arabian jasmine), Chameli (Spanish jasmine), *Kaminee* (Orange jessamine), *Kanakchanpa* (Maple twist), *Kunda* (Kund-jasmine), *Madhabee* (madhabi), *Rajaneegandha* (Tuberose), *Shephali* (Night jasmine) and *Sneuti* (Himalayan musk rose) are white; *Lal Shimul* (Red silk cotton), *Raktojaba* (China rose, red), Raktokarabee (Red oleander), *Raktokamal* (Red lotus), exhibit red or allied colour; *Neelshatadal* (Blue water lily) is blue; *Kadam* and *Sorshey* (Sarson) are yellow; *Bokul* (Indian medlar) and *Shireesh* (Siris) with greenish tinge; *Parul* (Trumpet flower) is violet or purple.

Another very attractive facet of flowers is their fragrance. *Golap* (Rose), *Rajaneegandha* (Tube rose), Beli (Arabian jasmine), *Chameli* (Spanish jasmine), and *Juin* (Jasmine) are flowers which have pleasing fragrance. Flowers of palash (Parrot tree) and *Shimul* (Silk cotton tree) are odourless. *Padma* (Lotus) and *Shaluk* (Water lily) with faint aroma add to the beauty of water areas around them. Some flowers bloom at night and others during daytime. Most of the day-blooming flowers have attractive colours, while those blossoming at night have intoxicating fragrance. Flowers with their bright colours and pleasing perfumes enchant poets, litterateurs and scientists alike, at the same time they attract insects and by causing pollination ensure that the plants continue to live on.

In conclusion, it might, perhaps be said that although ostensibly viewpoints of poets and scientists regarding flowers and plants differ in their basic approaches towards their utilization in their respective arenas, both unhesitatingly acknowledge that as a symbol of beauty, flowers are unique and unparalleled.

ASHATH-ASHATHWA-ASHWATH

(PIPAL, 'BO'-TREE)

"Roder belay ashath talay
ghaser porey asi
rakhal chheler moto kebal
bajai bosey banshi"

On a sun burnt day, sitting on grass under the pipal tree,
I play my flute like a cowherd"

A medium-to-large spreading tree indigenous to India and Myanmar and distributed almost everywhere in this subcontinent. It enjoys a very long span of life and is considered sacred to the Hindus and Buddhists. Religiosa, its specific name *(Ficus religiosa)* indicates 'pertaining to religion' or 'sacred'. It is one of the holiest trees in regions where Buddhism is the popular religion. Lord Buddha attained enlightenment under this tree. The tree attains a height of 10-15 m, a girth of 1-2 m with nearly horizontal spreading branches. Leaves are ovate or egg-shaped, broad, smooth, light in weight, very narrow at the apex, with shiny green upper surface, pendulous with slender petiole (8-10 cm) and flicker even with the slightest breeze. Such flickerings are rhythmical which increase with the velocity of wind making a rustling sound as in Tagore's lyric. On a moonlit night moonlight

is reflected from the glossy leaves. The tree becomes leafless for a short period by the end of winter but soon gets covered with pinkish leaves in spring turning to green on maturity. Flowers enclosed in spherical receptacles which develop into dark purple, stalkless fruits. When the fruits ripen, birds eat them up and start singing creating a pleasant eco-friendly environment.
The tree can grow and develop in any adverse condition and is planted along avenues and roadsides to provide shade to pedestrians. The bark, roots and juice of twigs are known to have medicinal properties. It is propagated by seeds and also through the excreta of birds dropped on roofs and walls of buildings and crevices of other trees.

Part	*Song number*	*Original song*	*Relevant line*
Prakriti	112	*Andharo ambare prachanda dambaru*	*Ashathwa pallabe ashanta hillol*
	139	*Saghana gahano ratri*	*Ashathwa pallabe brishti jharia*
	238	*Bakulgandhey banya elo*	*Ashoke ashwathe*
Kalmrigaya	—*scene v*	*Chal chal bhai*	*Ei* ashathtalay
Balmeeki Prativa	*scene iv*	*Chal chal bhai*	*Ei* ashathtalay

* In Tagore's Gitabitan (unabridged edition), entire song compositions are grouped under various heads or parts viz, Pooja/Spiritual (617), Swadesh / Patriotism (46), Prem/Love (395), Prakriti/Nature (283), Bichitra / Variety (138) and so on with separate running song number in each part. Again, in Prakriti out of 283 compositions, 9(1-9) are general and others specifically related to the six seasons of a year in Bengal, viz, 16 (10-25) on summer followed successively by 115(26-140) on monsoon, 30(141-170) on autumn, 5(171-175) on late autumn (Hemanta in Bengali), 12 (176-187) on winter and 96(188-283) on spring. Figures in brackets above ( ) indicate total number of songs listed in each part.

ASHOK, BANJUL
(ASOKA TREE)

"Bon hote keno gelo ashokamanjaree
phalguner angan shoonya kori"

Why have floral spikes of Asoka disappeared from the grove
robbing the spring courtyard of its delight?

A medium-sized evergreen, ornamental flowering tree found in India since early days and also native to Myanmar, Sri Lanka and Malaysia. It is widely grown in the gardens surrounding temples and monasteries for its majestic flowers. The word *ashoka* in Bengali implies "sorrowless" and the tree is considered a symbol of love and passion. The bloom is known to represent one of those five flowers that constitute the five arrows of Kamadeva, the god of love. In ancient India, most of the flowering trees were sanctified by the Aryans and offered to various gods and goddesses – 'Kadamba' to Lord Krishna, 'Silk cotton' (Simul) to Lord Siva, 'Blue Lotus' to Lord Vishnu and 'Asoka' to Kamadeva or the god of love. In Tagore's dance drama *Shyama*, the court dancer Shyama has been compared with a cluster of Asoka blooms as she was the symbol of youth, love and passion. As such when she was found missing from the royal palace, the *Kotal* (city guard) initially exclaimed as a police chief that she had to be

brought back at any cost but later uttered in a pensive mood – as someone who admired beauty, why did the Asoka blooms leave the joyous grove creating a complete vacuum in the spring courtyard? The *Kotal's* lamentation has been revealed in the relevant lines of scene iv of the drama which run as follows:
"Bon hotey keno gelo Ashoka manjaree, Phalguner angan shoonya kori."
The tree attains a height of about 4-5 m or more with spreading branches and rounded crown. Young leaves drooping, coppery red in colour turning to dark green on maturity and divided into five-six pairs of narrow, wavy-edged pointed leaflets. Flowers are very compact in dense clusters, orange-red to orange-yellow changing to vermilion, fragrant and are mostly noticed in early or late spring from March to May. Hairlike filaments of stamens, 2.5 to 3 cm long, six-eight in number shows orange near the base and scarlet upwards. With all these compact floral characters the tree looks extremely beautiful when in profuse bloom.
Like Ashwathwa (Pipal tree) Asoka is also considered a holy and sacred tree to the Hindus and Buddhists — it is immensely associated with Indian art and religion. A section of Buddhists would think that Lord Buddha was born under an Asoka tree, while others hold that it was a Palas (Parrot tree). In the Ramayana, it has been stated that Sita was kept captive by Ravana in the Ashok Kanan or an enclosure with Asoka trees. Foliage and flowers of the tree were very popular in Mathura sculpture in ancient times when tree motifs and women found place in red sandstones. Hindu women drink water in which six of such flowers are put and in Bengal, women eat flower buds on Ashok Sasthi, the sixth day in the month of Chaitra in spring season for protection of their children from worries and grief. Sometimes the tree is planted along avenues and its seeds, barks, roots, leaves, flowers and fruits are used as medicine. The plant regenerates by seeds and cuttings.

Part	*Song number*	*Original song*	*Relevant line*
Pooja	7	Tomar beena amar manomajhe	Tomar sur *ashok* shakhe arun renurage
Prem	194	Ogo amar chira-achena Paradeshee	Chhilo porhe trinadale *ashok*-bone
	215	Gopan kathati rabe na gopane	Madhur bedanaya alok piyasi *ashok* munjarila
	224	Basanta se jay to hese	Alak hote parhbe *ashok* bidaytahle
	230	Adhara madhuree	Bigata basanter *ashok* raktarage
	334	Ore chitrarekhadore	Elo chhanda murati kar naba-*ashoke*
Prakriti	195	Ananter banee tumi	*Banjul*nikunjataley sancharibey leelachhaley
	197	Orey grihabasee	Ranga hasi rashi rashi *ashokey* palashey
	233	Charanarekha taba	*Ashok* renuguli rangalo jar dhuli
	238	Bakulgandhe banya elo	Palash-Jabaye kanak chanpay *ashokey* ashwathey
	240	An go tora	Rakta ronger jagla pralap *ashok* gachhey
	241	Phagun, haoay *haoay*	Tomar *ashokey* kingshukey
	271	Amar malar phuler daley	An madhabee malatee a*shok* manjaree Shukabey banjul manjaree
	276	Ei kathatai chhilem bhuley	*Ashok* boney amar hiya
Bichitra	83	Je kabal paliye bedai	O ki tar uttareeya *Ashok* shakhay uthla duli
	100	Amra nootan joubaneri doot	*Ashok* boner ranga neshaye rangi

Part	*Song number*	*Original song*	*Relevant line*
Chitrangada	5	Laho laho phirey laho	*Ashok* boney hey anangadeb
	6	Trishnar shanti	*Ashoker* shakha gheri ballaree-bandhan

AM, AMRA, AMUA, SAHAKAR

(MANGO)

"Basanta aolo re ! Madhukar gun gun, amua manjaree kanana chhaola re"

The spring has arrived, bees are humming and the grove displays a jubilant exuberance of floral bunches of mango

A large spreading evergreen fruit tree of medium height (5-15m) which originates from Indo-Malaysian region is extensively grown in various parts of India. Since Vedic period this tree occupies an important place in day-to-day life of the people and is intimately associated with their religion, custom, art and culture. It is a sacred tree to the Hindus and on any festive or religious occasion their houses are decorated with its leaves. Water filled pots with mango leaves at the top are kept on entry door and leaves hung over the gates and doors are considered auspicious. The tree is mentioned in the two epics of the Hindus – the Ramayana and the Mahabharata. The flowers are known to represent one of the five arrows of the god of love. Mention of Am and some other ornamental plants viz. Ashok, Kunda, Madhabee, Neelpadma, Shireesh, Doorba and Chandan are made in Kalidasa's *Avijnana Shakuntala*.

The tree has a dense rounded or globular crown of dark green foliage. Leaves leathery, long and narrow, tapering at both ends with wavy edges. Young leaves often pink, coppery red or bronze hanging vertically downwards turning to green with age. Flowers are small, yellowish, strongly scented, unisexual or bisexual mixed in the same inflorescence. The tree looks very attractive with new leaves and flowers. Flowering starts from end of January to March and fruits ripen from May to July. The tree is universally acclaimed for its edible fruits which have also a number of medicinal uses. It is propagated by seeds, grafting (organic union between two plant parts) and sometimes by cuttings.

Part	*Song number*	*Original song*	*Relevant line*
Pooja	580	Chhinna patar sajai taranee	Sakaley dharano *amer* mukul
Swadesh	1	Amar sonar Bangla	O ma, phaguney tor *amer* boney
Prem	3	Kahar galay parabi ganer ratanhar	*Amer* shakhatey nootan mukul
	40	Ajana khanir nootan monir genthechhi har	Jemon nootan *amer* mukul
	77	Chapala taba nabeen ankhiduti	*Amer* bol, jhauer dol
	232	Ogo pardoshini	Klanto kujan dinasheshey *amrashakhey*
	298	Gahana ghana boney	Piyal tamal *sahakar* chhaye
Prakriti	40	Akashtaley daley daley	Jamer boney *amer* boney rob uthechhe tai
	63	Oi-je jhaera megher koley	*Amey* jamey shireesh shale
	191	Enechho oi shireesh bakul	Enechho oi shireesh bakul *amer* mukul
	192	O manjaree	O manjaree, o manjaree *amer* manjaree
	193	Kar jeno ei moner bedan	*Amer* boler gandhe mishe

Part	*Song number*	*Original song*	*Relevant line*
	201	Ami pathbhola ek pathik esechhi	Ami *amer* manjaree
	239	Basantee, hey bhubanamohinee	Shyama prantarey *amra* chhaye
	247	Chaley jay mori hay	Pulakita *amra*beethi
	250	Klanta jakhan *amra*kolir kal	Klanta jakhan *amra*kolir kal
	252	Aji ei gandhabidhura sameeraney	Aji *amra*mukula saugandhey
	275	Biday niye giyechhilem	Amra amer mukul go
Bhanusingher Padabalee	1	Basanta aola re!	*Amua*manjaree kanana chhaola rey
Natygeeti	115	Prahara shesher aloy ranga	*Amer* boney dola lagey
	128	Bahir holem ami	*Amer* mukul phutey phutey

AMLOKEE/AMLOKI

(AMLA, EMBLIC MYROBALAN)

"Sheeter haoar laglo nachan
amlokir ei dale dale "

The winter wind sets up a dancing impulse in twigs and branches of amla trees.

The beauty of this medium-sized deciduous tree lies in its numerous small, narrow, thin leaflets arranged in two opposite rows exhibiting rhythmic swing even with the slightest breeze. It is a native of tropical and subtropical India, Sri Lanka, China and widely distributed in almost every region of India. Hindus consider it as a sacred tree. Eating under this tree on "Akshaya Navami" festival day is considered auspicious by a large section of people.

The tree usually attains a height of about 5-10 m. It becomes leafless in autumn and new leaves and small greenish yellow flowers are borne profusely in spring and summer in the months of March-April. Round fleshy fruits are green when young turning to pale yellow or pink when ripe. Fruits appear in winter. Very smooth plum-like fruits mature in 10-11 months and may remain on the tree even after leaf fall till the next flowering.

Amla fruits are acidic in taste being one of the richest sources of vitamin C. The fruit juice is known to have 20 times more vitamin C than orange juice. Since ancient days the fruit is highly valued for its medicinal use. These are one of the ingredients of Ayurvedic "Chyavanprasha" and "Triphala". Fruits are also preserved as pickles. The plant is cultivated in the gardens and homeyards mainly for fruit. It is propagated by seeds, cuttings and air-layering or gootee.

Part	*Song number*	*Original song*	*Relevant line*
Prem	173	Keno amay pagol korey jas	*Amloki* bon maran-mata
Prakriti	176	Sheeter haoar laglo nachan	*Amlokir* ei daley daley
	185	Sheetere boney kon se kathin	*Amloki*-dal sajlo kangal
Bichitra	41	Amader Santiniketan	Sadai patar nachey metey achhe *amloki-kanan*

AMRHA

(HOG-PLUM)

The tree is not planted in the garden as ornamental plant but mainly for its edible fruit. It has its origin probably in the South Pacific Islands growing wild or cultivated in various parts of India, in forests and elsewhere.

It is a small -to- medium-sized tree, 3-4 m in height with smooth and aromatic bark. Very prominently veined large leaves emit smell of mango leaves when crushed. Flowers are small, yellowish- white and borne in leafless condition during March-April. The fleshy and edible fruit is acidic and found in December-January.

The plant is sometimes used as hedge plant and the fruit is used for pickles, chutneys and other preserves. The bark extract is used for tan. It is propagated by seeds and cuttings.

KACHU

(ARUM)

This perennial herbaceous plant with fleshy swelling underground stem is a native to South-Central Asia, perhaps in India and Malaysia, growing extensively in the moist and marshy places, in forests and sometimes in homeyards in the kitchen gardens for edible rootstocks, young leaves and stalks. It has nearly 1000 varieties.

The plant is conspicuous by its very big arrow-shaped leaves borne on long petioles and found in clusters. Creamy white flowers arise from the centre of leaf clusters. It is propagated by suckers and division of rhizomes.

KADAMBA, KADAM, NEEPA

(KADAM)

"Badal-diner pratham kadam phul korechho dan,
ami ditey esechhi shraboner gan
- .
- .
Aj enediley, hoyto dibey na kal
rikto habe jey tomar phuler dal."

You have gifted me the first flush of kadamba flowers of rainy days. I have come to offer you songs of shravana. (second month of the rainy season in Bengal) You find them for me today but may fail tomorrow as by that time the floral twigs may lose all their flowers.

Kadam, a tall fast-growing ornamental tree is admired throughout India, primarily for its golden ball of delicately scented flowers often compared with the smell of fresh wine and also for its mythological background. It is one of the most beautiful objects in nature. It is believed that in ancient times, nearly 2,000 years ago, vast tracts of Kadamba forests existed near Vrindaban region and Lord Krishna used to play the flute under those trees on the bank of the Yamuna river. In the Mahabharata there is mention of kadamba trees in Kamyak forest and the existing trees in Mathura are probably remnants of this ancient forest. In Kalidasa's *Meghduta*, women of the city of Alaka were described as holding a lotus in hand, putting on a shireesha flower in ear and kadamba flowers for parting of hair. Tagore's kadamba as expressed in his lyrics is unique for its colourful scented flowers symbolizing joy, sorrow, love and aspirations of people during monsoon.

The tree is native to India, China and South-East Asia, and widely distributed in the moist deciduous forests of India. It attains a height of 10-20 m with horizontal branches forming a dense crown of foliage with deep green leaves, 10-20 cm long. Young plants have larger leaves, green above and lighter below, broad and good looking, which are shed during winter. Numerous ball-shaped flowers, 4-5 cm across, borne on flower heads on 3-4 cm long peduncles at the end of twigs, are yellowish white changing to light orange blooming with the advent of the rains. The plant is propagated by seeds.

Part	*Song number*	*Original song*	*Relevant line*
Prem	39	Hey nirupama	*Nabakadamba* madir gandhey akul kore
	111	Tomar moner ekti katha	Sandhya mukharita jhillisware *neepa* kunjataley
	140	Sey asey dheere	Bikacha *neepa*kunje
	258	Neelanjana chhaya	*Prafulla Kadmbabon*
	266	Shrabanera pabaney	*Neepabona* gandhaghana andhakarey
	367	Ekhano tarey chokhey dekhini	*Kadamtaley jey khushi* sey chay
Prakriti	27	Oi asey oi oti	*Kadambarenu bichhaiya* dao shayane
	38	Ogo amar shraban megher	Pulak laga ei kadamber ekti kebal saji

Part	*Song number*	*Original song*	*Relevant line*
	41	Kadamberi kanan gheri	*Kadamberi* kanan gheri ashadh megher chhaya kheley
	53	Ahawban asila mahotsabey	*Kadambera* pallabey pallabey
	55	Neelanjanaghana punjachhayay	*Kadambabon* gabheer magan
Prakriti	60	Ei shrabaner buker	Sei aguner pulak phutey *kadambabon* rongiye uthey
	77	Badal-dhara holo sara	*Kadamkeshar* dhekechhe aj
	79	Eso neepoboney chhayabeethitaley	Eso *neepoboney* chhayabeethitaley
	89	Taper taper bandhan katuk	Phutuk sonar *kadambaphul* nibid harshaney
	92	Shraban, tumi batasey kar	Kadam jharey, hay hay hay
	93	Keno pantha e chanchalata	Kesharakeerna kadambaboney
	99	Eso heyeso	Byathiya uthey *neeper* bon pulak bhara phuley,
	102	Dharanee, doorey cheye keno	Ghirechhis mathay basan *kadamer* kusumdorey
	104	Madhu-gandhe-bhara	*Neepa*-kunja-taley
	110	Aji pallibalika shakhaye dulichhe	Aji *neepa* shakhaye pushpadola
	112	Andhara ambarey	*Kadambakunjer* sugandha madira
	118	Aji barishana mukharita	*Neepaboney* pulak jagay
	126	Badal-diner pratham *kadam* phul	Badal-diner pratham *kadam* phul

Part	*Song number*	*Original song*	*Relevant line*
	133	Esechhiley tabu aso nai	Pichhaney *neepabeethikay* roudra chhaya jay khele
Prem O Prakriti	97	Eso eso ogo shyamachhayaghana din	Naba *neepa*kunja nivritey

KANAKCHANPA

(MAPLE TWIST)

"Sheeter dine kanakchanpa
jay na dekha gachhe,
ghumer modhye nukiye thake
nei tabuo achhe"

Flowers of maple twist tree (kanakchanpa) are not seen in winter, they hide in slumber – exist, though not visible.

This medium-to-tall, majestic, evergreen flowering tree is a native to Indo-Myanmar region and distributed in Meghalaya, Manipur, West Bengal, Orissa and Karnataka.
The tree is admired for its height (10-15 m), leaf and flower characters. Leaves are very large, about 12-20 cm long and 10-15 cm broad, with tough, thick, lobes at the margin; the upper surface is dark green, and the lower surface whitish or greyish brown. Flowers are large, solitary or in pairs. The outer covering of sweetly scented flowers is composed of 5 long and very narrow thick fleshy segments about 10-12 cm long, which curl backwards with opening of flowers, five petals are pure white. Fruits contain numerous seeds with brown papery wing. Flowering occurs in spring and early summer and the scent is retained for a long time even after they are dry. Fruits on maturity in a year split allowing

seeds to float away by wind. Plant population is also increased by seeds.

Besides its use as ornamental and avenue plant, the tree is quite common around holy places of the Hindus, Muslims and Christians. Dropped flowers at the tree bases are excellent natural offerings to divine sites. The plant has also several other uses. The leaves are treated as country plates and bark and flowers contain medicinal properties. Flowers serve as general tonic for rejuvenation and as insect repellant for clothes.

Part	*Song number*	*Original song*	*Relevant line*
Pooja	2	Surer guru	*Kanakchanpa* kaney kaney
Prem	288	Tumi amaye dekechhiley	Chaila rabi shesh chaoa tar *kanakchanpar* boney
Prakriti	238	Bakulgandhey banya elo	Palash jabay *kanakchanpay*

KARABEE

(OLEANDER, ROSE BAY)

Karabee is small-to-medium sized, beautiful, evergreen, flowering shrub native to India, Iran, Mediterranean regions and Japan. It is cultivated in Indian gardens as an ornamental plant and is common in templeyards, courtyards, residential gardens and traffic islands. The plant exhibits various shades of flower colour – red, white, pink or rose.

The plant attains a height of 2-4 m with long, slender, upright branches. Leaves are thick and arranged in pairs or whorls. Flowers are funnel shaped with pleasant smell, visible almost throughout the year, more in summer, autumn and winter. Flowers are mostly single in wild condition, but in cultivation semi-double or double forms are predominant.

Karabee is one of the most favourite flowers of Tagore. To him red oleander (Raktakarabee) is the symbol of love, beauty, vitality, freshness and all such real expressions of life. The plant is associated with his symbolic love drama *Raktakarabee*, a tribute to this flower.

Besides serving as a good, decorative garden plant, its stems, leaves and flowers are known to have medicinal properties. It is propagated by seeds, cuttings and gootie.

Part	*Song number*	*Original song*	*Relevant line*
Prem	12	Nidrahara rater e gan	Alakey tar ekti guchhi *karabeephul* raktaruchi
	53	Ami chahitey esechhi	Sharamey jarhita kato na golap kato na garabi *karabee*
	169	Keno re etai jabar twara	Shithil *karabee* brintajhara
	220	Ogo kishor, aji tomar dware	Ano go ano bhariya dali *karabeemala* loye
Prakriti	27	Oi ase oi oti	Ksheen kotitate ganthi loye paro k*arabee*
	173	Hemonte kon basanteri banee	Shwet *karabeer* akal jagarone
	201	Ami pathbhola ek pathik	Ami tarun *karabee*
	219	Sahasa dalpala tor	O chanpa, O *karabee* !
	230	Ebar bidaybelar sur dharo	O chanpa, O *karabee* !
	243	He madhabee, dwidha keno	*Karabee* diyechhe sarha
	271	Amar malar phuler dale achhe lekha	An *karabee* rangan kanchan
Natyageeti	130	Ei to bhara holo phule phule	*Karabee* rupaseer alakananda

KANCHAN

(MOUNTAIN EBONY)

In his poem 'Sheshdan' (last offering), the poet expresses his feelings in a pensive mood for a kanchan tree (mountain ebony) standing isolated in the boys' play ground at Santiniketan which runs as follows:

"Chheleder khelar prangan
* * *
ek dhare achhe kanchan gach,
apon ranger mil pai na se kothao
* * *
kanchan gach ache eka dwanarhiye,
apon shyamal prithibeete noi,
manusher paye dala garib dhulor pore.
* * *
Tar hasimukher bedona
phute uthlo bhare bhare
phike begunee phule.
Pata gelo na dekha,
jatoi jhare tatai phote,
hate rakhlo na kichhui.
Tar sab dan ek basante dile ujarh kore."

English abstract: A mountain ebony tree stands isolated in the boys' play ground. It does not have harmony of colour anywhere. The tree stands alone not on this green earth but in a neglected corner of the ground getting trampled all over.. Magnificent display of light mauve flowers is a manifestation of its pain and affliction of the smiling face. Leaves missing, more the floral droppings more its exuberance of bloom. Nothing kept reserved. It exhausted all its treasures in a single spell of spring.

Usually six species of Bauhinia grown in gardens or elsewhere are broadly known as kanchan. Among these three, viz. *B. acuminata* (Shwet *kanchan), B. purpurea (Deb kanchan) and B. variegata (Rakto-kanchan)* are widely grown in the gardens and most exclusively termed as 'Kanchan' by plant lovers. The plants originate from India and the lower slopes of the Himalayas.
These plants have distinct bilobed leaves resembling camel's hoof. *Bauhinia acuminata* is a tall shrub, about 3 m in height and with snow white flowers from March – September. *Bauhinia purpurea* is the tallest among the three, a 10-16 m tree, almost evergreen, producing flowers in shades of purple, white and crimson during early winter, in October. *Bauhinia variegata* is small- to- medium sized deciduous tree, 5 – 8 m in height with leaves 6 – 8 cm across, somewhat broader than long which are shed in winter. From the end of January till March (late winter), the tree is laden all over with large fragrant orchid-like flowers in various shades of purple, pink or red gradually covering the leafless branches. At this time the plant appears as one of the most beautiful gifts of nature. The flowering continues up to the entire spring season. Use of kanchan along with Kingshuk (Flame of the forest), Karabee (Oleander) and Rangan (Torch plant) by Tagore in his lyric, suggests that he had Rakto Chandan (*B. variegata*) in his mind during such compositions. The following indications will make it amply clear. .... "No sooner than the winter had disappeared, the kanchan has bloomed. There is no end to its profusion. It seems the entire garden is vibrant with its loud laughter. In the garden, it is the first to catch the eye.)" (Ref: Ghosh, P.K. *et al, Tagore and flowers*, 1993, p. 17).
Apart from ornamentation and decoration, these have various other uses – economic and medicinal. The roots of raktokanchan

are commonly believed to be a cure for snakebite. This tree is also sacred to the Buddhists as it has found place in Buddhist culture. Propagation of *Bauhinia* is done by seeds and gootie.

Part	*Song number*	*Original song*	*Relevant line*
Prem	45	He sakha barata peyechhi	Dekha dao *kingshuke kanchane*
Prakriti	271	Amar malar phuler dale achhe lekha	An karabee rangan *kanchan*

KAMINEE

(CHINESE BOX, ORANGE JESSAMINE)

"Tora khela kar, tora khela kar kaminee kusum guli
kabhu pata majhe lukaye mukh, kabhu
baiyu kachhe khule de buk,
matha narhi narhi nach kabhu nach
baiyu kole duli duli"

English translation:

"Play, play o' floral clusters of kamini, go on playing
incessantly Sometimes hide faces behind the leaves,
at times open your heart to the rough waves of the
wind, occasionally resort to dancing by swinging in the
lap of breeze oscillating your head gently."

Kaminee is tall, beautiful, ornamental flowering shrub or a small tree, native of India and South East Asia and distributed in most of the gardens of this sub-continent.

This evergreen plant, 2.5-4 m high, has numerous dark green, glossy leaves with 5-9 leaflets. Sweetly scented flowers in small clusters at sides and branch ends are visible almost throughout the year, more during late summer and the rains. Fruits are initially green but turn to conspicuously small or orange red berries on maturity.

Kaminee is popular not only for its ornamental value but for several other reasons. It is a unique specimen of ornamental hedges planted for screening and for decorative topiary work. Leaves and barks are known to have medicinal properties. It is propagated by seeds, cuttings and air layerings (gootie).

Part	*Song number*	*Original song*	*Relevant line*
Prem	105	Noopura beje jay	*Kaminee phulkul barashichhe*
	124	Keno jaminee na jete	*Kaminee* shithil saje
Prem	188	Ke amare jeno	Ei to phutechhe pataye *kaminee* guli
	349	Kee holo amar	Amar moner k*aminee* paprhi
Prakriti	275	Biday niye giyechhilem	Tumi ke go 'k*amineephul'*
Natyageeti	9	Khela kar, khela kar tora	*Kamineekusumguli*

KASH

(THATCH GRASS)

"Kasher hasi haoay bhasi
jay je chale"

English abstract :

(Expecting arrival of winter) Jubilation of kash is over and the flowers are drifted away by the current of winter waves.

Shiuli (Night jasmine), Kash (Thatch grass) and dew drops are the forerunners of autumn. This season never attains its grandeur in Bengal unless kash is in profuse bloom in the state. After a dull and gloomy monsoon, autumn brings relief to people and gives them ample joy and pleasure. Whiteness and rhythmic gentle swing of long floral heads of kash flowers with blowing breeze express this jubilation.

It is a perennial grass, 2-3 m high with narrow grass-like leaves widely distributed in India, Sri Lanka, Australia and Southern Europe. In India, it is found in groups along river banks and in vacant and fallow lands making a forest-like look. The plant is known in this subcontinent since ancient days and finds its place in Kalidasa's composition.

Soft, woolly, silvery-white flowers are borne in pyramid like inflorescence known as panicle, 30 cm or more in length.

Freshness and whiteness of flowers fades out with the advent of late autumn, (Hemanta in Bengali) and continues up to winter. During this period, exceedingly light flowers float in the surrounding area following the air current. Most of the lyrics on kash imply end of monsoon and advent of autumn or winter. Kash is used to check soil erosion, in paper industry and for thatching village huts. It is also a good sand binder and fodder crop. Propagated by stem cuttings and suckers.

Part	*Song number*	*Original song*	*Relevant line*
Prem	23	*Chhutir banshi bajlo*	Akash hase shubhra *kasher* andolane
Prakriti	40	Akashtale dale dale	*Kasher* bone kshane kshane rob uthechhe tai
	96	Chale chhalo chhalo nadeedhara	*Kasher* bone bone dulichhe kshane kshane
	144	Amra bendhechhi *kasher* guchchha	Amra bendhechhi *kasher* guchchha
	171	Himera rate oi gaganer	*Kash* jhore jay nadeer teere
	185	Sheeter bone kon se kathin	*Kasher* hasi haoay bhasi
Prem O Prakriti	76	Charanarekha tabo	*Kasher* shikha jato kanpichhe tharothari

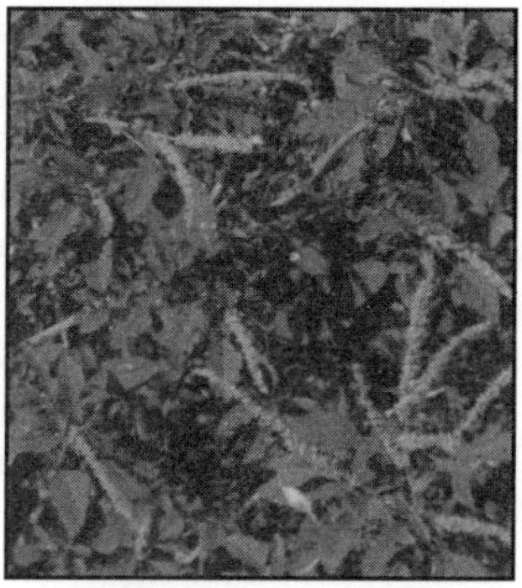

KANTALATA

(THORNY WEEDS)

*"Payer kachhe ekti kantikari (Kantalata)
antaranga kachher sanga tari, doorer shoonye
apanare se prachar
nahi kare. Matir kachhe nata hole pare
snigdha sarha dei se dhulishayan theke
neelbaraner phuler buke ektukhani
sonar bindu enke."*

English translation :

*A Kantikari (thorny weed) is there close to my feet with all its charm and warmth of intimacy. It does not announce its presence
in a loud voice. When stooping down to the ground, its affectionate response can be felt from the bed of dust by its spectacular display
of a tiny golden dot on the bosom of its blue flowers.*

Specific identity of Kantalata in Tagore's composition is not properly exposed. In lyric, the term has been used only once to specify thorny, weed-infested areas left unattended for a long period. Sometimes it appears that it may be kantanotey, the prickly Amaranth (*Amaranthus spinosus*), a small thorny herb

cr Shiakanta, the thorny Mimosa (*Mimosa rubicaulis*), a small bushy, thorny shrub with minute, hairy, violet flowers turning to white later. The possibility of kantikari or yellow berried night shade (*Solanum surattense*) is also not ruled out, as specific mention of this plant is found in Tagore's poem with identical name (Kantikari) in 'Parishesh' and 'Balai' in Galpaguchha (a collection of short stories). The plant is a herb with thorns all over the stems and lobed leaves with five- petalled white or blue flowers, bearing golden dots at the centre during summer.
All such plants are growing as weeds in the open and unused places needing eradication for betterment of site.

Part	*Song number*	*Original song*	*Relevant line*
Bichitra	13	Jakhan padbeyna mor payer chinha	*Kantalata* uthbey gharer dwargulay

KUSUM

(LAC TREE, SAFFLOWER, FLOWER)

Schleichera oleosa (Lac tree or Honey tree) and *Carthamus tinctorius* (Safflower), the two species of plants of dissimilar nature are popularly known as 'kusum' in Bengal, though sometimes the term specifies flowers in general, in this part. Tagore in his lyrics has used kusum several times, indicating flowers on some occasions and sometimes as two plants as stated above. A brief account of these plants are given below:

Schleichera oleosa, the Lac tree, attains a height of 15-20 m and a girth of 2-3 m. It is a native of India and Sri Lanka and distributed in the states of Bihar, Madhya Pradesh, Karnataka and some regions of Bengal, in forests or large gardens.

The beauty of this plant lies in its elegant height and new leaves. Leaves are shed in winter. With the advent of spring new leaves of bright red colour emerge, often mistaken as flowers which on maturity turn green. The large sized compound leaves also add beauty to the plant. Flowers in small clusters, greenish or yellowish are found in late spring or early summer. Fruits are edible.

The plant serves more as a forest tree rather than an ornamental plant. It acts as a host to lac insects. Barks and seeds have medicinal value. It is propagated by seeds.

Carthamus tinctorius, Safflower is a small, erect, annual herbaceous plant up to 1 m in height. It is in cultivation in various states of India and is probably a native of Afghanistan, India and extending throughout the world.

The plant bears single, alternate leaves with spines at margin and narrow apex. Flowers are pretty, initially yellowish turning to orange red, borne in globular heads and found during winter and spring.

It is mainly cultivated as oil seed crop. Flowers are used as dye for colouring food and clothes. It is propagated by seeds.

To understand which of these three kusums Tagore has used in a particular lyric, one has to go through the relevant lines very carefully and the revelation will be automatic.

Part	*Song number*	*Original song*	*Relevant line*
Puja	77	Tumi je cheye akash bhorey	Phaguner *kusum* achho phota habey phanki
	175	Ei molin bastra chharhte hobey	Sandhyaboner *kusum* tuley
	474	Tumi dhanya dhanya hey	*Kusum*bon chhaile shyam pallabey
	519	Mor sandhaye tumi	Ei gandhagahana sandhya-*kusum* malate
	538	Chiradibasa taba madhuree	Naba *kusuma* pallaba, naba geeta, naba ananda
	541	Prabhatey bimala anandey	Bikashita *kusuma* gandhey
Prem	30	Sabar sathey chaltechhila	Chena *kusum* phutey achhe na chena ei gahan boner dharey
	37	Kato katha tarey chhilo bolitey	Se katha phutia uthey *kusuma* boney (Katha tarey chhilo bolitey)
	38	Sunil sagarer shyamal kinarey	*Kusum* kunje se pabaney dulibey
	61	Sakhee, pratidin hai ese phire jai ke	Tare amar mathar ekti *kusum* de

Part	*Song number*	*Original song*	*Relevant line*
Prem	63	Tomar gopan kathati	Jabe suptimagana bihaganeerh *kusum* kananey
	120	Man abhiman bhasiye diye	Shushka *kusum* parhchhe jhorey
	153	Akul keshey asey	*Kusum* suravi mridu paboney Byakul basana *kusum* kananey
	192	Amar praner parey chole gelo ke	Apan-money bosey achhi *kusum* bonetey
	224	Basanta se jay to hesey	Shesh *kusumer* parash rakhey)
	255	Bone jadi phutla	Boney jadi phutla *kusum*
	300	Ogo ke jay	*Kusumer* mala gantha holo na
	317	Oli bar bar phirey jai	Aji bihaga rajanee phulla *kusuma* shishira saliley bhasey
	354	Sukhe achhi sukhe achhi sakha	Gopone tulia *kusuma* ganthia rekhe jabey malagachhi
	359	Jeo na jeo na phirey	Chanchala sameera sama phirichho keno *kusumey kusumey* kananey kananey
	383	Biday karechho jarey	Aji madhu sameeraney nisheethey *kusuma* boney Mukulita dashadishi *kusumadaley*
Prakriti	2	*Kusumey kusumey* charan chinha diye jao	*Kusumey kusumey* charan chinha diye jao
	168	Sei to tomar pather bnodhu	Door *kusumer* gandha ene khonjay madhu

Part	*Song number*	*Original song*	*Relevant line*
	205	Akash amay bhorlo aloy	Dakhin haoay *kusum* boner buker kanpon thamey na je
	227	Biday jakhan chaibe tumi	Pata-jhara *kusum* jhara nikunja kutirey
	270	Madhura basanta esechhey	*Kusum* tulichhey phutaye
Bichitra	66	Ore sabdhani pathik	Jharey pordey achhe kantatarutaley rakta *kusum* guchha
	67	Taree amar hathat dubey jay	Lagbe taree *kusumboney* chhilem sei ashay
	105	Kothay phiris param shesher anweshaney	Tari chhnona legechhe oi *kusumboney*
Bhanusingher padabalee	2	Shuno lo shuno lo balika	Rakha *kusuma* malika, Dulai *kusuma* munjari, *Kusumahara* bhailo bhara
	8	Gahana *kusuma* kunja	Gahana *kusuma* kunja majhey
	11	Aju, sakhi, muhu muhu	Shihare tanu jarajara *kusumabono* majha
Natyageeti	2	Hridaye rakho go debee	Bishanna *kusuma* kula banaphul boney
	40	Amader sakhirey ke niye jabey rey	Bendhe tay rekhe debo *kusumboney*
Pooja O Prarthana	19	Rajanee pohailo	*Kusum* phutechhe boney
Prem O Prakriti	5	Boli, o amar golap-bala	*Kusumakunja* karo ala
	71	Tumi to sei jabei chole	Ele amar *kusum* bone

KRISHNAKALI, SANDHYA PHUL, SANDHYAKALI, SANDHYAMALATI

(FOUR-O'CLOCK PLANT)

Krishnakali, the Four-O'clock plant is a dwarf, bushy, ornamental, perennial, tuberous rooted herb which originates from tropical America and is distributed in various parts of India, including Manipur, West Bengal and North West Himalayas. As its flowers unfold in the evening, the plant is known as Four-O'clock plant in English and sandhyaphul, sandhyakali, sandhyamalati in Bengali. (Sandhya = evening).

Plants form a bush and attain a height of about 1 m. Leaves are small and betel-like (5-6 cm). Krishnakail flowers are clustered, fragrant, resembling the shape of oleander flowers, with the long and narrow (3-4 cm) base and undivided petals with colour ranging from red, white, yellow, violet and even with mixed coloured stripes. The plant blooms profusely during summer and the rains and increase its number by seeds and root tubers of the previous year.

Although grown in gardens as an ornamental plant, it grows uncared for along roadsides, not getting its due regard, recognition and appreciation by busy pedestrians. Krishnakali flowers are a source of a dye, and seeds, roots and leaves have medicinal properties.

Tagore's 'Krishnakali' is a dark-complexioned girl whom he adores for her inherent beauty. Her lyrical name is also probably after this flower which grows very often in gardens and roadsides, often uncared for and unnoticed, blooming at a time when sunlight starts receding and darkness begins. It is vibrant with its rustic natural beauty caring little for admiration from any source.

Part	*Song number*	*Original song*	*Relevant line*
Pooja	47	Ebar amay dakle doore	Amar *sandhya-phuler* madhu
	99	Bajao amare bajao	*Sandhyamalati* saje je chhande
Bichitra	75	Krishnakali ami tarei boli	*Krishnakali* ami tarei boli

KRISHNACHUDA

(PEACOCK FLOWER, BARBADOS PRIDE)

Krishnachuda is beautiful, tall, bushy ornamental shrub with widespread branches reaching a height of about 3 m. The plant is native to West Indies and distributed in the gardens of the tropics.

The beauty of the plant lies both in its leaves and flowers. Compound bipinnate leaves (25-30 cm) are divided into small, dark green, lacy looking, oblong leaflets (1.5 - 2 cm) borne on branches (pinnae) of the midrib, each pinna bearing 8 – 12 pairs of such tiny leaflets. Orange-scarlet flowers in 20 – 30 cm long panicles with long, slender, bright scarlet stamens in terminal ends are in bloom almost throughout the year, mostly during summer and monsoon. Flowers are pleasantly scented and invite butterflies and other insects. Base of the inflorescence with fully open flowers and the top with yet-to-open floral buds reminds the shape of mythological peacock crown of Lord Krishna (*Kanhar Mor Mukut* in Hindi, *Krishna's Mayur Mukut* in Bengali). Rosea and Flava – two varieties of this plant with rosy-red and bright yellow flowers respectively— are common ornamental flowering specimens in the gardens. Of these Flava is popularly called Radhachuda. These are multiplied by seeds and cuttings of young shoots.

Some authors, however, mention *Delonix regia*, a very popular ornamental flowering tree of the same family, as Krishnachuda.

It is native to Madagascar and bears orchid- like flowers in clusters at branch ends blooming in summer and monsoon when branches and leaves are less. These plants with flowers in various shades of scarlet, yellow, orange and maroon, are beautiful specimens for gardens and avenues. These are increased by seeds. Most authors are inclined to mention *Caesalpinia pulcherrima* as Krishnachuda, its variety Flava as Radhachuda and *Delonix regia* as Gol Mohor, Gul Mohar or Flamboyant.

Part	*Song number*	*Original song*	*Relevant line*
Prakriti	208	Eto din je bosechhilem	Karne tomar *krishnachurhar* manjaree
	226	Aj dakhina batase	*Krishnachuda* churhay saje

KEYA, KETOKEE

(SCREWPINE)

"Sahaj sadhan labdha nahe se mugdher nibedan,
antare aiswaryarashi, achchhadane kathor bedan"
(Tagore, Rabindranath, Parichay (Mahua),
Rabindra Rachanabali vol II (1982, p. 794)

English version:

It is not easily accessible to its admirers. It has immense treasures within, well guarded by outer cover, so much painful.

The plant is famous for bearing one of the most odorous flowers in the world. It is a native of old world tropics and grows abundantly along sea coasts, canals, river banks, low lying fields, wet lands, as also in forests, parks and gardens. It is a source of keorha essence, a commercial perfume known since ancient times and also an essential oil. It has earned due recognition in Kalidasa's literature. The identity of the plant can easily be traced even from a distance and in the midst of a bush encircled by other plants for its extremely sweet scented flowers which last for several days. Tagore in his lyric appreciates Keya for its inherent wealth and qualities which at the same time restrict intimate approach of others with its deeply serrated leaf margins.

Keya is thickly branched evergreen tree reaching a height of 4 – 6 m. Several such plants in groups form a dense bush and a forest-like look. The stem is supported by aerial adventitious roots arising from the lower part of the main trunk and grow obliquely downwards penetrating the soil. Leaves are long and narrow (1 – 2 m), in bunched clusters on stem tops, deep or light green in colour with serrated margins usually twisted in spirals. Male and female flowers are borne on different individuals. The inflorescence of the male flower (spadix) in dense terminal clusters is encircled by large, white, sweetly scented bracts (spathe). The green, light green or white coloured bracts are a combined form of sepals and petals and look like small country boats. Female flowers (spadix) scented, in solitary clusters encircled by whitish leaves, stigma short and uniformly yellow. Flowering occurs during late spring to the rains. Flowers may appear even at 25 years. Fruits are edible— initially green turning to red or yellowish red on maturity, much alike those of pineapple. The plant increases by seeds and suckers.

Part	*Song number*	*Original song*	*Relevant line*
Pooja	28	Jatakhan tumi amay	Shraban diner *keya*
Prakriti	27	Oi asey oi oti	*Ketokee keshare* kesh pash karo suravi
	43	Chhaya ghanaichhe	Gopane gopane eli *keya*
	45	Shrabanbarishan par hoye	Gopan *ketokeer* parimaley
	77	Badal-dhara holo sara	Moumachhira *keyaboner* path giyechhe bhuli
	86	Ekla bosey badal-sheshey	'Ebar, amar gelo bela' bole *ketokee*
	92	Shraban tumi batasey kar abhas peley	*Keya* kande, 'jay jay jay'
	123	Mor bhabonare kee haoay	Jal bheja *ketokeer* door subasey

Part	*Song number*	*Original song*	*Relevant line*
	125	Ogo snaotali chhele,	*Keyaphoolkhani* kabe tule ani
	140	Ogo tumi panchadashee,	Pratham asharher *ketokee* saurabh
	142	Megher kole rod hesechhe,	*Keyapatar* nouko godey sajiye debo phuley

GOLAKCHANPA

(PAGODA TREE)

Golakchanpa is a cultivated species of *Plumeria*, a native of tropical America, with fairly scented flowers and colours ranging from red, white, pink, rose, etc. It is popularly known as Frangipani (a perfume in France named after its inventor), Pagoda tree, Temple tree, Gulancha, etc. among people of different regions. The tree is acclaimed as a symbol of eternal life and commonly found in gardens, near temples, tombs and monasteries considering its holiness and purity.

It is a small- to- medium sized deciduous tree, 4 – 8 m in height, with round and fleshy stem, shiny bark, spreading branches and full of milky juice or latex. Leaves are large (25 – 30 cm), lance shaped or round tipped (as per individuality), prominently veined and densely crowded at branch ends. Leaf fall starts in winter and leafless condition of the tree persists up to the beginning of the rainy season. Before monsoon floral buds often appear in phases even before leaf emergence. Flowers are large (5 – 8 cm), variable in colour and expressions. In *Plumeria rubra* (Red Frangipani) profuse blooming is observed from February – October, corresponding to early spring and late autumn with intermittent flowering in winter. In another type (*Plumeria acuminata*), the flower is white with yellow eye. Blooming continues one after another, persists in clusters for a few days, then get detached from the clusters in ones or twos and cover the tree bases. Tagore in his lyric uses Golakchanpa only once and that too on this observation.

The tree bears long, cylindrical, pendulous pods (fruits) in pairs which are often seedless. Leaves and milky latex are known to possess medicinal properties. Propagated easily from stem cuttings in spring.

Part	*Song number*	*Original song*	*Relevant line*
Prem	69	Ekla bose hero tomar chhabi	Tapto haoay shithil manjari *golokchanpa* ekti duti kori payer kachhe padchhe jhari jhari tomare nandiya

GOLAP

(ROSE)

"Amar bondhu jakhan ratrisheshe
parash tare korbe ese,
phuriye giye dalguli sab
charaney tar lutbe

When my friend will touch it gently at night end, the petals feeling exhausted will sprawl on the ground at his feet.

Rose is universally acclaimed as the 'Queen of Flowers' because of its elegant shape, very sweet and appealing fragrance and a wide variety of choicest and fascinating colours. Beauty, dignity and aristocracy of its flowers have been cherished and appreciated by plant lovers all over the world for thousands of years. It has been a symbol of love and adoration from time immemorial. The earliest reference of rose in ancient India has been cited in *Viswakosha*, an encyclopedia in Bengali. Mention is also there in Ayurveda by *Charaka* around 1000 AD.
About 120 known wild species – all indigenous to temperate regions of northern hemispheres. [illegible]mber of hybrids and varieties are known. Modern roses are supposed to have derived from Chinese and European roses. The Persian rose, particularly the Damask rose, was introduced in India during the early Mughal period.

It is a perennial ornamental, thorny, bushy, flowering shrub. A climber variety is also there. Its leaves are pinnately compound, alternate with oval and serrated leaflets. Flowers may be single, semi-double and double with numerous odorous (sometimes without odour) petals in various colours, shapes and sizes. Flowers have changing forms at bud stages and open flowers with variable number and texture of petals. Buds bloom slowly and gradually. Flowering excellence is observed during winter and spring, though blooming occurs occasionally in other seasons.

In lyrical expressions, Tagore believes that all his agonies, sorrow and pains in real life alike thorns of rose in its body, would ultimately bring joy, success and prosperity similar to blooming roses. Like the moon in the sky, the morning dewdrops and all other natural phenomenon, the poet is also waiting anxiously to find a rose bud developing to a fully open flower. Dropping of rose petals has also its own rhythm. Petals stick to fully open flowers loosely which drop with passing air current or by gentle touch of darkness at night.

Flowers have also immense domestic, aesthetic and commercial uses. Floral extracts yield an essential oil used in 'rose water' and 'attar'. Petals were used by women in early days while taking bath and for self decoration. The plant is propagated by cutting, layering, budding and grafting.

Given below are two familiar desires of roses:

1. "We dislike being badly handled and mauled; beauty is to see and not to touch". — K. Bhattacharjee, Rosy Dream, The Indian Rose Annual (IX), 1991, 154 (Sl.4).
2. "If you consider us queen of flowers, please protect our dignity and privacy like in a palace" — Ibid, p.159 (Sl.7)

Part	*Song number*	*Original song*	*Relevant line*
Pooja	293	Amar sakal kanta dhanya korey	Sakal byatha rangin hoye *golap* hoye uthbe
Prem	53	Ami chahite esechhi	Katona *golap* katona garabi
	394	Bal, *golap*, morey bal	Bal, *golap*, morey bal

Part	*Song number*	*Original song*	*Relevant line*
Prakriti	282	Phagun haoay rongey rongey	*Golap*-jaba parul
Natyageeti	130	Ei to bhara holo phule phule	*Golape golape* miliya miliya
Prem O Prakriti	5	Boli, o amar *golap*-bala	Boli, o amar *golap*-bala
	6	*Golap* phul phutiye achhe	*Golap* phul phutiye achhe

CHANDAN

(SANDALWOOD TREE)

"Aha shwetchandan tilake
aji tomare sajaye dila ke"

English abstract :

O dear! Who has put the ornamental shwetchandan
(white sandalwood) on your body to make
you so beautiful?

By the Bengali word 'Chandan' three distinct botanical species of dissimilar nature are indicated: (1) *Santalum album*, the white sandalwood tree as 'Shwetchandan', (2) *Pterocarpus santalinus,* the red sandalwood tree as 'Raktachandan' and (3) *Adenanthera pavonina*, the coralwood tree as 'Ku-chandan' or 'Raktakambal'. In lyric however, Tagore's focus of attention is obviously on 'Shwetchandan'. It is a small evergreen tree, native of the mountainous parts of the Malabar coasts in South India and grown in some gardens of tropical countries.

White sandalwood tree with spherical heads attains a height of about 5–6 m. The tree bears numerous tiny leaves (5–7 cm) and inconspicuous flowers on terminal and lateral panicles. Flowers, initially straw coloured and changing to purple afterwards, are visible almost throughout the year. Fruits are globose, smooth and black when ripe.

Since ancient days sandalwood paste, sandalwood dust, sandalwood pieces have been in use by the Hindus as an auspicious symbol in almost all of their ceremonial functions – social and religious. Almost every part of the tree – the wood, the root and the seeds are of high economic and commercial value. Sandalwood oil obtained from its 'heart wood', sandal wood powder, sandalwood sticks, are all extremely favourite decorative articles. Because of overexploitation its population has been alarmingly reduced and it is now considered as a rare and threatened species in India. The tree is propagated by seeds and young seedlings are parasitic in nature.
It has been expressed in lyric that autumn sky displaying tiny, white patches of clouds seems to be decorated with white sandalwood paste.

Part	*Song number*	*Original song*	*Relevant line*
Pooja	378	Rakho rakho re jeebane	Akulia dao pran gandha *chandaney*
	588	Rajaneer shesh tara	Nabadiney *chandaney* kumkumey
	612	Dukkha je tor noi re chirantan	Bhorbe thalay mala o *chandan*
Prem	32	Sundar hridiranjan tumi	Laho hridayer *phulachandan* bandan upahar
	34	Bhalobese sakhee nibhritey jataney	Ekti bindu enko tomar lalata *chandaney*
	94	Chander hasir bandh bhengechhe	Neel gaganer lalatkhani *chandaney* aj makha
	170	Jani jani holo jabar ayojan	Porbe bhale mangala*chandan*
Prakriti	150	Ogo shephalibonera monera kamana	Aha *shwet chandan* tilake
	199	Ogo bodhu sundaree	Chandineer *chandan*
Natyageeti	111	Bajo re banshori, bajo	*Chandan* malye mangala sandhay sajo
	112	Tomay sajabo jataney	Kumkuma *chandane*

CHANPA, CHAMPAK, CHAMPA

(GOLDEN CHAMPA)

"Champa" is medium sized evergreen tree with cylindrical or conical crown indigenous to lower hill regions of India and Malaysia. In Sanskrit it is known as 'Champaca'. Since ancient time it has been appreciated by the poets for beauty and fragrance of flowers. It is grown in gardens, near temples and in other places of meditation, popularly termed as *tapobans* in those days. At present its population is less in West Bengal though found in Assam and Tripura to a greater extent. It is considered as a very sacred tree in many regions of India. Hindu women have special regard for the species. Its flowers are sometimes thought to be divine and offered by a section of devotees to Lord Vishnu. In Tagore's lyrics there has been frequent mention of this flower, its appealing colour and scent, which in spring and monsoon reminds past memories.

In cultivated form, the tree attains a height of about 6 – 15 m with straight and round bole. Leaves are simple, alternate, entire, ovate lanceolate, 20 – 25 cm long, 5 – 10 cm broad tapering at the end, smooth, shining above, margins often wavy and pale green in colour. Leaf buds are covered with deciduous stipules. Flowers are nearly 5 cm across, solitary and borne in axils of leaves. Its perianth (fusion of two floral parts – sepals and petals)is 9 - 15 in number, fleshy, pale yellow, brown yellow or dull orange in colour, strongly scented, outer perianth is oblong and inner linear; stamens are long and numerous. Initially light yellow coloured flower buds look like flame of an earthen lamp which unfold gradually. It has been cited in the lyric in an inimitable and unique fashion. ["*Jetha chanpa koraker shikha jwale*". Tagore, Rabindranath, "*Prakriti" (Basanta), Akhanda Gitabitan, 1999, p 519].* Fruits are in long clusters of capsules and seeds reddish turning to brown hanging in thread- like structures.

Besides serving as an ornamental plant the tree has several other uses. From time immemorial the flowers have been inspiring poets, philosophers and literary personalities. An essential oil commonly known is 'Chanpa oil' is obtained from flowers which is in use in perfumery industry for perfumed hair oil and *attars*. Roots, barks, flowers and fruits have medicinal properties. The plant is raised from fresh seeds and stem cuttings and the seedlings bear in 3-4 years.

Besides Golden champa Swarna chanpa, botanically known as *Michelia champaca*, eight other different species of plants are also known as various forms of Chanpa in Bengali and other Indian languages. These are:

1. Kanak chanpa (*Pterospermum acerifolium*)
2. Muchkund chanpa (*Pterospermum suberifolium*)
3. Dulichanpa (*Magnolia pterocarpa*)
4. Kath chanpa (*Plumeria rubra*)
5. Ramdhan chanpa (*Ochna jabotapita*)
6. Dolon chanpa (*Hedychium coronarium*)
7. Bhuin chanpa (*Kaempferia rotunda*)
8. Kanthali chanpa (*Artabotrys uncinatus*)

Most of these plants have been used separately in Tagore lyrics, the first four are large or medium-sized trees, the fifth one is a shrub, the sixth and the seventh are herbs and the eighth one is a scandent shrub. In a very appealing and well-composed early Bengali story for children there has been a mention of seven brothers in a forest, all known by Chanpa and Parul (*Stereospermum colais*), their only sister. The reason for calling all such plants as c*hanpa* is not clearly understood, when these are mostly of dissimilar natures and structures and belonging to different families. Probablities may be to their ornamental behaviour or sweetly scented perianths or their probable earliest common origin in Chanpa regions of the country. But these are all mere assumptions.

Part	*Song number*	*Original song*	*Relevant line*
Pooja	28	Jatakhan tumi amay	Phagun diner bakul chanpa
	30	*Ganer jharna talay*	*Je* sur *chanpar* peyala bhorey
	127	Sarthaka karo sadhana,	*Champakabon* karuk rachana naba kusumanjalika
	7	Ganer dali bhorey de go	*Chanpar* koli *chanpar* gachhe surer ashay cheye achhe
	45	He sakha, barata peyechhi	Dekha dao *champakey* ranganey
	188	Ke amare jeno enechhe dakiya,	*Chanpa* kotha hotey enechhe dhoriya
Prem	293	Ekada tumi, priye,	Phagun ajo je re khunje phere *chanpa phule*
Prakriti	19	Baishakher ei bhorer haoya	*Chanpaboner* kanpan chhale
	23	Madhadiner bijan batayane	Sara belaye, *chanpar* chhayay chhayay
	31	Shanwana gagane ghora ghanaghata	Bilunthita lola chikura mama bandhana *champaka* male
	142	Megher kole	Makhba gaye phuler renu *chanpar* boney luti
	149	Aj pratham phuler	*Chanpa* bhayer shakha chhayer tale
	198	Ektuku chhnoa lage	Kichhu ba *chanpay* mesha
	199	Ogo bodhu sundaree	Pulakita *champar* laho abhinandan

Part	*Song number*	*Original song*	*Relevant line*
	219	Sahasa dalpala tor	O *chanpa*, O karabee!
	230	Ebar bidaybelar sur dharo	O *chanpa*, O karabee !
	232	Aj ki tahar barata	Jetha *chanpa* koraker shikha jwaley
Bichitra	80	Ogo nadee, apan begey	Ami stabdha *chanpar* taru
	94	Pakhee baley,	*Chanpa*, amare kao
Natyageeti	111	Bajo re, banshori, bajo,	*Champaka* anganey photey ni ki ajo
	130	Ei to bhara holo	*Champa* chameli seunli beli
	132	Kothao amar hariye jaoar	Parulboner *champa re* mor hoy jana
Prem O Prakriti	6	Golap phul phutiye achhe,	Hethay bela, hothay *chanpa*

JABA

(CHINA ROSE)

Jaba is an excellent and very popular evergreen flowering shrub native of China and tropical Asia. Indian parks and gardens are never complete without a specimen of this plant. A large number of its hybrids and mutants are grown throughout the world. The flowers have high religious value. Loose flowers and garlands especially of red colours are offered during pujas to goddess Kali by a section of the Hindu devotees. Tagore has also expressed such feelings in one of his lyrics.

The plant attains a height of 2–4 m. Leaves are smooth, alternate, ovate, serrated, narrow at tip and deep green in colour. Flowers are small to large, solitary on long peduncles, axillary, single, semi-double or double, in different shades of colour including red, pink, yellow, white, violet and others. Blooming occurs almost throughout the year, sometimes in great profusion.

The flowers are a source of a dye used in shoe polish and sometimes used as medicine against broncheal ailments. It is propagated by stem cuttings, budding and graftings.

Part	*Song number*	*Original song*	*Relevant line*
Prakriti	238	Bakulgandhe banya elo	Palash *jabay* kanakchanpay ashoke ashwathe
	282	Phagun haoay ronge ronge	Golap *jaba* parul palash parijater buker pare

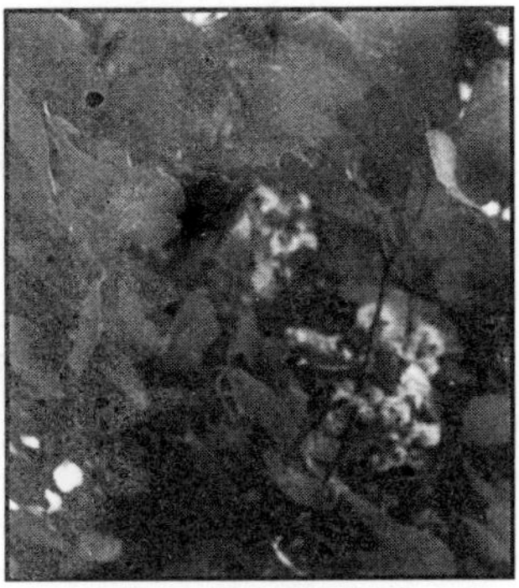

JAM, JAMBU

(INDIAN BLACK BERRY, JAVA PLUM)

Jam is a tall, evergreen tree with many branches, native of the tropics and growing wild in forests and also in cultivated forms in gardens for edible fruits. It is one of the most favourite plants of Tagore because of its wild appearance, a forest -like look when in groups, a canopy of green foliage and its ability to provide shade and shelter. In his lyric, the tree finds place only in songs related to the rainy season. In his poem 'Meghdoot' (Manasee) the tree is specified as Jambu. In the song '*Neelanjana chhaya'* (Prem, p 258) the relevant line '*Jambupunje shyam bonante'* (2) also refers to this tree. Jam is known to be dear to gods Ganesha and Shiva. It is frequently visited by birds and monkeys because of numerous leaves and hanging branches.

The tree reaches a height of 8–15 m. Leaves are 10–15 cm long and of varying shape and sizes, the apex being abruptly narrow. New leaves appear during spring. Flowers are small and greenish white in colour borne in open clusters on long stalks from branches below the leaves during March to June. Fruits are small, shining, sizes vary from a pea to a plum, initially red turning to violet later and finally black on ripening during summer to the early rains— pulp juicy and palatable.

The tree is planted along roadsides, in parks and gardens as windbreaks and providing shade. Flowers are a source of a kind of honey and juice from unripe fruits and are used for making vinegar. *Tassore silk* worms are also known to rear on this tree. It is propagated by seeds, airlayering and grafting.

Part	*Song number*	*Original song*	*Relevant line*
Prakriti	40	Akashtale dale dale	*Jamer* boney amer bone rob uthechhe tai
	63	Oi je jharhera megher kole	Ame *jame* shireesh shale
	72	Badal baul bajay re ektara	*Jamer* bone dhaner kshete

JNUI JATEEYA PHUL

(JASMINES)

There are about 15,000 species of flowering plants in India out of which only 67 have been used by Tagore in his lyrics which again includes seven different species and varieties of *Jasminum*. These are Kunda, Chameli, Juthee, Banmallika, Bela, Mallika and Malati. *Jasminum* which is derived from an Arabic name includes about 200 species of shrubs, climbers and climbing shrubs bearing attractive flowers, mostly fragrant and grown in tropical and sub-tropical parts of Asia, Europe, Africa and the Pacific regions. Nomenclature of species of *Jasminum* is very confusing and needs extensive studies for authentic stabilization particularly those in cultivation. Species recorded from India differ slightly from one another and some may be varieties or cultivated forms of a few such species. Even among many popular species in cultivation many are simply horticultural selections based on size of flowers and aroma. Among those bearing fragrant flowers, three or four species are of commercial importance being sources of cut flowers or for extraction of perfumery oil. These are *Jasminum auriculatum, Jasminum flexile, Jasminum grandiflorum and Jasminum sambac.* Species and varieties with widely accepted nomenclature have been used to specify *Jasminum* species referred to in Tagore's composition.

Tagore's special fascinations for flowers of *Jasminum* have been revealed in his song compositions. The reasons may be probably due to their two exclusive appeal —— whiteness in colour which is also a symbol of purity and a very pleasant appealing aroma. Excepting "Malati", Tagore used flowers of other jasmine group of plants viz. Jnui, Beli, Chameli, Mallika, Kunda and Banmallika for seventy-three times in his song compositions.

KUNDA

(KUND-JASMINE)

This attractive, dwarf, evergreen, floriferous climbing shrub is very intimately associated with Indian civilization. It is a native of India and tropical Asia and is common in almost every garden in our country. Tagore is impressed with its blooming excellence, whiteness and decorative value which are clearly expressed in his lyrics "*prem*"(53), "*prakriti*"(170) and again in "*prem*"(166), respectively.

The plant with rambling growth attains a height of 1.5 to 2 m. Leaves are simple, opposite, ovate (3–5 cm), upper surface without hair but pubescent beneath. Large, glorious white, fragrant flowers (3 cm across), single or double, are borne in profusion at the tip of short, lateral, pendulous branches, corolla tube slender, 7-9 lobed. Blooming excellence is found from autumn to spring which may extend even up to summer. Roots, leaves and flowers have medicinal uses. Flowers are also used for making floral ornaments. It is propagated by cuttings and suckers.

The variety *Rubescens* has drooping branches and bushy growth, leaves being narrower than those of Kunda – Jasmine. Flowers have white inner surface and pink outer surface borne during winter, mostly from January to March. It is propagated by cuttings and ground layerings.

Part	*Song number*	*Original song*	*Relevant line*
Prem	53	Ami chahitey esechhi	Anek *kunda* anek shephali bhorechhe tomar dala
	166	Sakalbelar aloy bajey	Kunder dul seemontey
Prakriti	170	Naba kunda dhabaladala	Naba *kunda dhabaladala* susheetala
	187	He sannyasee, himgiri phele	*Kundamalatee* korichhe minati'
	235	Tomar asan patba kothay	Chhilo phute malateephul *kundakoli'*

CHAMELI, JATI

(SPANISH JASMINE)

"Ami pathbhola ek pathik esechhi.
Sandhyabelar chameli go
sakalbelar mallika,
amay cheno ki"

English abstract :

A stray traveller is here. Dear Chameli (Spanish Jasmine)
of dusk and Mallika (Malli Jasmine) of dawn,
am I known to you?

Kunda–jasmine is famous for its excellent white colour but Spanish jasmine is adored for its pleasing fragrance, dusty white colour of flowers and flush of nocturnal bloom. The lyrics also highlight its floral qualities – fragrance, colour and bloom in spring to monsoon nights.

It is an ornamental climbing shrub native to India and distributed mostly in North Western regions. Its leaves are oppositely arranged. Flowers are star shaped, dusty white, fragrant, borne in clusters almost throughout the year, profusely during summer and the rains. Flowers purify the environment and are used for preparation of *attar* and perfumed hair oils, garlands and hair decoration.

Much alike Spanish jasmine, there is one other plant species popularly known as White jasmine (Juin in Bengali) also a climbing shrub bearing spotless, milky white, fragrant flowers during night. It is very difficult to distinguish the two species unless the leaflets are noted. A comparative analogy of these two is given below.

Name	*Flower*	*Scent*	*Scientific name*	*number of leaflets*
Spanish jasmine	Comparatively large	Comparatively more	Jasminum grandiflorum	7 - 11
White jasmine	Comparatively small	Comparatively less	Jasminum officinale	3 - 7

Both the plants originate from India with almost identical floral qualities. Both are propagated by cuttings.

Another small, bushy, ornamental, non-jasmine shrub upto 1.5 m in height, native of India, is also known as 'Jati' or 'Jnati' in Bengali. This plant is botanically known as *Barleria cristata* and in English as 'Philippine violet' bearing dull green leaves and tubular, violet or purplish-blue flowers in clusters from the rains to early winter. Some are of the opinion that the Bengali name 'Jati' has been coined by Tagore. (Ghosh, P.K. *et al*, *Tagore and Flowers*, 1993, 54). But it has been ascertained from Tagore's writing that he came to know later that 'Jati' and 'Chameli' specify the same plant. Thus the plant under reference is better known as 'Jnati' and not 'Jati'. It is used in gardens for decoration and making hedges. It has a variety which bears white flowers. Propagateion is from cuttings.

Part	*Song number*	*Original song*	*Relevant line*
Prem	187	Ohey sundara mamo grihe aji	Sakal kunjakanan phiri enechhi joothee *jati*
	253	Tomara geeti jagalo smriti	Badal sheshe karun hese jeno *chameli*-kaliya

Part	*Song number*	*Original song*	*Relevant line*
Prakriti	201	Ami pathbhola ek pathik esechhi	Sandhyabelar *chameli* go, sakal belar mallika
	237	Mon je boley chini chini	Chaitrarater *chamelirey*
	242	Nibirh ama timir hotey	Alor mala *chameli* baranee
	243	He madhabee, dwidha keno	Chamaki uthilo jagi *Chameli* nayan meli thore'
Bhanusingher padabalee	5	Sajani sajani radhika lo,	Mallika *chameli* beli Gnatha joothi gnatha *jati*
	8	Gahana kusuma kunja majhey	Bakula joothi *jati* re
Natyageeti	130	Ei to bhara holo phule phule	Champa *chameli* Sneuti beli
Prem O Prakriti	96	Nirjan ratey nihshabda charanpatey	*Chamelir* ingit asey jey batasey

JOOTHEE, JUNTHI, JNUI

(JNUI-JASMINE)

"Esechhile jeebaner ananda dootika
sahasa tomare jabe korilo haran
nirmal maran
pareni korite tabu churi
tarun praner tabo karun madhuree
ajo rekhe gechhe tar charam sourav
chittaloke smritir gourab"

English abstract :

You were here as a harbinger of the joys of life but when you were taken away suddenly by innocent death; it failed to steel the pensive charm of your young vibrant life which has left behind your excellent fragrance and infuses my mind with glorious recollections — even today.

Not only in songs and poems, Joothee or Juin has a warm and affectionate place in the day-to-day life of Bengal and is so popular among gardeners and plant lovers that the climber hardly needs any introduction. It grows easily in the prevailing soil and climate and purify the air all around by its presence, especially when in bloom. While growing in a solitary corner of a residence, it becomes a live companion of the family throughout the year and shares its joy and sorrow. It serves as a source of unending pleasure during post- afternoon periods when darkness descends during spring, summer and the rains in its full bloom stages.

It is a bushy and woody climber native to India. Its leaves are single or trifoliate. Numerous small (1.5 cm), star-like, white, fragrant flowers are borne in clusters in terminal ends from March to September. The plant is propagated by cuttings and ground layerings.

In Tagore songs, the flowers are used for its fragrance, ornamental and decorative qualities, for making garlands and the like. Joothee's smell — sad and sorrowful — reminds one in pensive mood, memories of those distantly located who cannot be reached in spite of strong desire. Along with such grief-stricken expressions in lyrics, the plant also reveals joy and pleasure though the former expressions dominate.

In a letter written to Dinendranath Tagore from Buenos Aires on December 20th, 1924, Rabindranath expressed his love and affection for Juin after getting completely overwhelmed by a feeling of a known fragrance which reminded him of sweet memories of his homeland. His nostalgic mood is reflected in his poem "C*hithi*" *(Purabee)* as given below:

[*Rabindra Rachanabali* vol II, 1982, p. 684]

"Swapnasama parabase eli pashe kotha hote tui
O amar Jnui"

(Far far away from my homeland you are now here in my dreams, my dear Juin! Where have you come from ?)

Besides ornamental and decorative value, the flowers are used in religious and ceremonial functions. Ladies find pleasure in decorating their hair with Juin flowers. The flowers also yield an essential oil required in perfumery industry and are in use for making various floral crafts.

Part	*Song number*	*Original song*	*Relevant line*
Pooja	568	Ebar rangiye gelo	*Sandhyajootheer* gandha bhare
Prem	13	Amar kantha hotey	Megher dine shrabanmase *jootheeboner* deerghaswase
	39	He nirupama	Tabo kunchita keshe *jootheera* mala
	170	Jani, jani holo jabar ayojan —	*Jootheeboner* phuljhara krandan
	175	Klanta banshir shesh raginee	Jhara *jootheer* pataye dhekey
	187	Ohe sundara, mamo grihe aji	Sakala kunja kanana phiri enechhi *joothee* jati
	197	Bajey karuna surey	*Joothee* gandha ashanta sameere
	277	Mone kee dwidha	Sikta *jootheera* gandha bedaney
	304	Kakhon je basanta gelo,	Ebar basante kirey *jootheeguli* jagenirey
	306	Pathik paran, chal, chal se pathey tui	Bikelbelar juin *Sandhyajootheer* swapanmoyee chhaya
Prakriti	23	Madhyadiner bijan batayane	Aj keno sei *bonjootheer* basey
	33	Asharh sandhya ghaniye elo,	Sajal haoa *jootheer* boney
	44	Ei shrabon-bela badal-jhara	*Jootheeboner* gandha bhara
	59	Ore jharh neme aye	*Jootheeboner* gandhabanee chhutla niruddeshey
	79	Eso neepabone chhaya beethitaley,	Kajalnayane, *joothee* mala galey

Part	*Song number*	*Original song*	*Relevant line*
Prakriti	81	Aj shrabaner poornimatey	*Joothiboner* bedan ase
	105	Ami takhan chhilem magan	Kunjabeethir sikta *jootheer* gandhe
	115	Mone holo jeno periye elem	Path hotey ami ganthiya enechhi sikta *jootheer* mala
	121	Kichhu balbo boley esechhilem,	*Jootheekunrhi* niye kole
	128	Eso go, jwele diye jao	*Joothee* malikar mridu gandhe
	214	Bakee ami rakhba na kichhui —	Ujad korey debo paye bakul bela *juin*
Bichitra	93	Adheka ghumey nayana chumey	Shranta valey *jootheera* maley
Chitrangada	1	Ore jhad nemey aye,	*Jootheeboner* gandhabanee
Bhanusingher Padabalee	5	Sajani sajani	Gantha *joothi*, gantha jati
	8	Gahana kusumkunjamajhe	Bakul *joothi* jatirey
Prem O Prakriti	85	Mone holo periye elem	Sikta *jootheer* mala

BANAMALLIKA

(WILD JASMINE)

Banamallika is a medium-sized, shrubby climber familiar in India since early days. It is grown in most of the gardens in tropical and sub-tropical regions, in various parts of India and more abundantly in South India.

The plant bears small, ovate leaves (2-3 cm), variable even on the same plant. The flowers are solitary or in threes, starshaped, white and very fragrant, corolla lobes 1.5-2 cm in diameter. Flowering normally occurs from late winter to summer, though blooming somewhat in other seasons may be found depending on the location.

In Tagore songs, Banmallika or Wild Jasmine has been used in relation to Kunja or bower which is a decorative garden feature in a selected enclosure where shade is provided by various flowering climbers like Banmallika and others. Tagore probably has in his mind one such exclusive enclosure by Wild Jasmine. These places are love nests for lovers during day time. Poet Joydev who flourished at the close of the 12th century in India, reveals the feelings of high romance in '*Geeta Govinda*' in such spots through his Sanskrit composition "*Chalo sakhi kunjam satimira punjam*", *i.e.,* let us go to the bower steeped in a mass of darkness.

The plant is used in verandah and garden decoration for its odorous flowers. Its roots and leaves have medicinal properties. The plant is propagated by cuttings.

Part	*Song number*	*Original song*	*Relevant line*
Prem	251	Rodanbhara e basanta	Kunjadwarey *banamallika*
Prakriti	202	Aji dakhin duar khola —	Eso *banamallika* kunje
Chitrangada	2	Rodanbhara e basanta	Kunjadwarey *banamallika*

BELA, BELI, BEL, BALLIKA

(ARABIAN JASMINE)

A dwarf, bushy, evergreen flowering shrub with pubescent branches, popularly known as Bela, Beli, Bel or Ballika, is a native of India and Arab countries and has been growing in Indian gardens since ancient times closely associated with Indian social life and culture. Frequent mention of this flower in Tagore's lyrical compositions and poetry has made it an object of his attachment to the plant and his love and appreciation for it.

The plant is about 1 m in height. The leaves are simple (4-8 cm), almost sessile, opposite, ovate, dark green in colour with wavy margin. The flowers are 1.5–3 cm across, single, semi-double or double, borne solitary or in 3–12 flowered clusters in terminal inflorescence (cymes). They start blooming during late spring and continue throughout the entire spring, summer and the rains. Fully open flowers are usually seen in the evening.

This plant includes a large number of horticultural forms. Double-flowered varieties are known as Motia or Mogra. The flowers are used in garlands, floral crafts, in social and religious functions and in perfumery industry.

Part	*Song number*	*Original song*	*Relevant line*
Prakriti	214	Baki ami rakhbo na kichhui —	Ujad korey debo paye bakul *bela* juin
	249	Amar mallikaboney	O mor karun *ballika*, O tor shranta mallika
Bhanusingher Padabalee	5	Sajani sajani Radhika lo,	Mallika chameli *beli*
Natyageeti	130	Ei to bhara holo phuley phuley	Champa chameli seunti *beli*
Prem O Prakriti	6	Golap phul phutiye achhe,	Hethaye *bela*, hothaye chanpa

MALLIKA, MALLI

(MALLI-JASMINE)

Beautiful and sweet scented Mallika blooms from monsoon to spring, mostly at late hours of the night. Some confusion might be there on its true botanical identity. Though many floriculturists consider it as a variety of Beli (*Jasminum sambac* var Mallika), some believe that Mallika and Beli are one and the same. In lyrical composition of Bhanusingher padabalee, use of *Mallika-Chameli-Beli* in the same line indicates that Tagore was aware of separate identities of Mallika and Beli. While fragrance of other jasmine flowers are messengers of romantic involvements with mixed feelings in human minds, the smell *of Mallika* has been cited in Tagore's lyrics as a source of joy and pleasure ("*Bichitra*",p 83). Morning bloom, fragrance and decorative value of flowers find place in such lyrics.
This variety has comparatively larger flowers. It is grown in gardens as an ornamental flowering shrub. Floral crafts made of these flowers are used by Indian women in decorating their hair and as a substitute for ornaments.

Part	*Song number*	*Original song*	*Relevant line*
Prem	107	Barshanamandrita andhakarey	Enechhi *mallika* manjaree
	233	Ogo swapnaswaru-pinee	Bikacha *malli* malye tomare smaria rekhechhi bharia dala
	279	Likhan tomar dhulay hoyechhe dhuli,	*Mallika* aji kananey kananey kato
Prakriti	174	Sedin amay bolechhiley	Bone *mallikar* mela
	189	Eso eso basanta, dharatoley	Manjula *mallika* malye
	195	Ananter banee tumi,	Milana *mallika* malya paraibey paranballabhey
	199	Ogo bodhu sundaree,	Mukulita *mallika*-malyer bandhan
	201	Ami pathbhola ek pathik	Sakalbelar *mallika*
	229	Na, jeyo na, jeyo nako,	*Mallika* oi jay chaley jay
	249	Amar *mallika*boney	Amar *mallika* boney O tor shranta *mallika*
	271	Amar malar phuler daley	An karabee rangan kanchan rajanee–gandha prafulla *mallika*
Bichitra	46	Alo amar alo ogo,	Alor dheuye uthlo neche *mallika* malatee
	83	Je kebol paliye bedaye,	*Mallikar* oi bhangeetey
Chitrangada	5	Eso' eso' basanta dharataley	Eso' manjul *mallika* malye
Bhanusingher Padabalee	5	Sajani sajani Radhika lo,	*Mallika* chameli beli
Natyageeti	82	Manomandira sundaree!	*Mallika* abalunthita!

MALATEE, MALATEELATA

(MALTI)

(Jasmine and other kind)

"Oyi Malateelata dole
piyal tarur kole"
("Prakriti", p. 111)

Many a time *Malatee* and Madhabee are grouped together in Tagore's lyrics probably because of their apparent structural behaviour, both being large, heavy, evergreen and woody climbers requiring some able support provided by solid tree stems or others for growth and development. Tagore thus writes:

The climber is botanically known as *Aganosma caryophyllata* which originates from tropical America and is very popular in warm, humid regions of India, Malay and South China. In India, it is common in West Bengal, Bihar and coastal regions of West and South India.

The plant develops many well- spread-out branches. Its leaves are large (7-12 cm), opposite, petiole, red- coloured veins. Flowers are numerous, small (2 cm), white, star-like and fragrant blooming profusely in clusters, mostly during summer and the rains, sometimes in other seasons too.

The plant is quick-growing and common in gardens on outer walls, pergolas and arches. In Santiniketan, arches near residential buildings of Tagore were known to be decorated with this plant.

Besides *Aganosma caryophyllata* any other large, ornamental climber of Jasmine known as *Jasminum flexile* (*J. azoricum*), is also called malatee. It is indigenous to India and East India and distributed in the North-Eastern and Southern states. It has opposite, trifoliate leaves, leaflets elliptic and acute, distinctly nerved. Its flowers are small (2 cm), white and fragrant, borne on axillary or terminal inflorescence (cyme) almost throughout the year, more in winter.

Both the plants have been used in Tagore's lyrics. Both contribute in beautifying gardens and both are propagated by cuttings and layers.

Part	*Song number*	*Original song*	*Relevant line*
Prem	23	Chhutir banshi bajlo	Jharey pada *Malatee* tar gandhashwase
	44	Jani jani tumi esechha	Oi to *Malatee* jhorey pade jaye
	52	Aji godhoolilaganey	Utala hoyechhe *Malateer* lata
	130	Ebar milan-haoaye haoaye	*Malatikar* mala gantho nabeen phuley
	174	Jadi holo jabar kshan	Boner prantey oi *Malateelata*
	305	Banshori bajatey chahi	Malin *Malateemala*,
	318	Doorer bandhu surer dooteere	Sajao jataney baraner dala *Malateer* mala,
Prakriti	27	Oi ase oi oti	*Malatee* malinee kotha priyo paricharika
	47	Gahana ratey shrabandhara	Na hoye rekho *Malateekoli*
	84	Dharaneer gaganer milaner chhandey	Badal batas matey *Malateer* gandhey
	93	Keno pantha, e chanchalata	*Malatee* tabo charaney pranata

Part	*Song number*	*Original song*	*Relevant line*
Prakriti	103	Hridaye mandrila damaru guru guru,	*Malatee ballaree* kanpay pallab
	111	Oi malateelata doley	Oi *Malateelata* doley
	116	Trishnar shanti, sundar kanti,	Jhillir mondrey *Malateer* gandhey
	119	Jaye din, Shraban din jaye	Sikta *Malatee* gandhe
	144	Amra bendhechhi kasher guchchha,	Jhara *malateer* phuley
	159	Dekho dekho, dekho, shukatara ankhi meli chay	*Malateer* boney boney
	162	Ebar abagunthana kholo	*Malatee* bitan taley bajuk bnodhur banshi
	169	Pohalo pohalo bibhaboree	Tuli nabo *Malatee* manjaree
	187	Hey sannyasee, himgiri phele	Kunda*malatee* karichhe minati
	189	Eso eso basanta, dharatale	Akool *Malatee* balli bitaney
	225	Tomar bas kotha je pathik	O Madhabee, O *Malatee* !
	235	Tomar asan patbo kothay	Chhila phutey *Malatee*phul kundakali
	271	Amar malar phuler daley	An Madhabee *Malatee* Ashok manjaree
Bichitra	9	Eso go nootan jeeban	Thak beena benu, *Malatee* malika
	46	Alo amar, alo ogo,	Alor dheuye uthlo neche Mallika *Malatee*
Chitrangada	6	Eso' eso' basanta	Phula-akul-*Malati*-balli-bitaney
Bhanusingher Padabalee	3	Hridyak sadh mishaol hridaye	*Malati*mala rakhaha bala

Part	*Song number*	*Original song*	*Relevant line*
Natyageeti	10	Andhar shakha ujal kari	Bijan boney, *malatee* bala
	20	Basanta prabhatey	Basanta prabhatey ek *Malateer* phul
	21	Tarutaley chhinnabrinta	Tarutale chhinnabrinta *Malateer* phul
	130	Ei to bhara holo phuley phuley	Naba-*Malatee* gandha dhala
Prem O Prakriti	76	Charanarekha tabo	Malina *Malatee* je parhichhe jhari jhari
	86	Jani jani esechha pathey	More anginay *Malatee* jharia podey jay
	87	Kee bedona mor jano	Karun parashey se *Malatee* bikashita
	88	Amar kee bedona seki jano	Sei *Malatee* aji bikashita
	98	Shraboner baridhara	Se phirey *Malatee*boney

JHAU

(CASUARINA, SHE-OAK)

"Brishtidharar jharojhare
Jhaubaganer moromare"

Incessant rain rustling among trees in casuarina groves

These thin-leaved plants in general, are inclined to swing in air but the rhythmic swing of branchlets of casuarina with blowing of gentle breeze, is something fascinating, very special and lyrical. Such spell of foliar vibration is often expressed in poems, lyrics and literary works — 'The soft sighing of the air through its innumerable slender twigs is a pleasant sound, reminiscent of the noise of the sea on a distant shore .' (Benthal, A.P., *The trees of Calcutta and Its Neighbourhood, 1946*). This is also the theme in Tagore's lyrics.
Casuarina is a large, evergreen tree which resembles a pine tree. It is a native of Australia, Pacific regions, Malay and Bangladesh and is distributed mainly along coastal areas of India.
The tree attains a height of about 30 m or more. Woody jointed branches end up in green branchlets which look like pine leaves (needles) but actually the tree is leafless. The leaves are represented by minute scales. Unisexual, male flowers produced at branch ends and female flowers as small spherical cones are visible in summer.

The tree is mostly used in outskirt plantation in gardens, as windbreaks, along avenues and seacoasts. It is also used in afforestation, reclamation of waste coastal areas and as fuel wood. The tree is propagated by seeds.

Part	*Song number*	*Original song*	*Relevant line*
Prem	69	Ekla bosey hero tomar chhabi	Ghater dharey kampita *jhau* shakhey
	73	Anek katha bolechhilem	Bristidharar jharo-jhare *Jhau* baganer maromarey
	77	Chapala tabo nabeena ankhi duti	Amer bol, *Jhauer* dol
Prakriti	241	Phagun, haoay haoay	Tomar *Jhauer* doley
Prem O Prakriti	63	Tarun prater arun akash	Nadeer dharer *Jhauguli*

JHUMKOLATA

(PASSION FLOWER)

"Jhumkor phul phote dale
choreo chay na kono kale,
kane jhumkor phul dami"

Even thieves never care to look at the floral twigs of passion flower (Jhumkolata) in bloom, but when in ear as earrings, they are highly precious.

Jhumkolata or passion flower represents a unique group of herbaceous or woody ornamental climbers of *Passiflora*, mostly native of tropical South America and cultivated in Indian gardens to a fair extent. They bear 3-5 lobed leaves and are extremely handsome, attractive, fragrant flowers, 6-10 cm across in various shades of blue, violet, red, etc. during summer and the rains. The name is probably due to the resemblance of its flowers with Jhumka or ladies' earrings when borne isolated on short floral branches bent with weight. In lyrics, the plant has been mentioned twice but without any reference of flower colour or any other distinguishing morphological characters of the plant. It is thus assumed that Tagore has not mentioned any particular species while using Jhumkolata.

Passiflora in cultivation in Indian gardens are as follows:

1) *Passiflora caerulea*:: This variety is a native of Brazil, popularly known as 'Blue passion flower'. It bears deliciously scented, lovely, blue, fragrant flowers, about 8 cm across, during monsoon. It is a vigorous and hardy climber for decoration and screening.
2) *Passiflora edulis*: This variety is also a native of Brazil, popularly known as 'Passion fruit'. It is a woody climber with serrated trilobed leaves and about 8 cm wide, white, showy flowers with purple tints blooming during summer and the rains—fruits are edible. It is an ornamental plant cultivated in commercial scale.
3) *Passiflora foetida*: Popularly known as 'Stinking passion flower'; it is herbaceous climber growing wild in several parts of India. It emits a strong offensive smell when bruised. Its leaves are trilobed. Flowers cut up into moss like gland-tipped pectinate segments — fruits are edible when ripe but poisonous in unripe condition. This plant is not a good ornamental species.
4) *Passiflora racemosa*: This variety is a native of South America, popularly known as the 'Red passion flower'. Its leaves are trilobed, beautifully green with tendrils in their axils— a slender projection helping the plant to climb. The flowers are deep red, blooming during summer and monsoon. Its fruits are delicately flavoured. It is a handsome flower for decorating arches and pergolas.
All these plants are propagated by seeds and cuttings.

Part	*Song number*	*Original song*	*Relevant line*
Prakriti	185	Sheeter boney kon se kathin	Tai to apan rong ghuchalo *jhum-kolata*
	193	Kar jeno ei moner bedan	*Jhumkolatar* chikan pata

TAMAL, TAMALEE

(EGG TREE)

"Shala-piyale tala tamaley
nibida timiramoya kunja"

A mass assemblage of Shal, Piyal, Tal and Tamal (sal, cuddapah almond, palmyra palm and egg tree) plunge the arbour in deep darkness.

A small-to-medium-sized bushy, umbrella-shaped, evergreen tree with dark black outer layer of trunk and dense, dark green, shining foliage, this tree is botanically known as *Garcinia xanthochymus* and is probably a native of India and Myanmar. It is intimately associated with legends related to Lord Krishna. There have been frequent mentions of the tree in the Krishna lore and also in 'Sanskrit, Pali and Vaisnaba literatures. In Sanskrit 'tama' indicates darkness and hence probably the name 'tamal'. Greater intensity of darkness during monsoon days creates a very romantic atmosphere surrounding the tree trunk and the colour reminds the Krishna devotees of Krishna's image. The tree is also very common in Agra, Mathura and adjoining districts of Uttar Pradesh known to be familiar with devotees of Lord Krishna.

Tamal attains a height of 6 m or more. Its leaves are narrow and pointed, 20-40 cm, deep blackish green, drooping with prominent midrib. Leaf shedding often occurs in autumn but new leaves quickly appear. Small, yellowish-white flowers (2 cm), in bunches of 4-8 in leaf axils, are found in spring (March-April). The fruit is oval or round with somewhat pointed apex, almost egg-shaped, deep yellow — edible when ripe.

Garcinia morella — another variety — is a medium-sized, evergreen tree, mostly restricted to Khasi and Jayantia hills of the North Eastern region, West Bengal and Western ghats, commonly known in English as 'Ceylon gamboge'. It has also been cited as *Tamal* in some literature. Its trunk is deep brown and not black and it produces greenish-white flowers. The two plants have also other marphological differences, though they belong to the same genus. Both the plants are propagated by seeds and cuttings.

Part	*Song number*	*Original song*	*Relevant line*
Prem	298	Gahan ghana boney	Piyal *Tamal* sahakar chhaye
	299	Ke uthey daki	Ghana *Tamal* shakha nidranjan makha
Prakriti	1	Bishwabeenarabey bishwajan mohichhe	Piyal *Tamal* bitaney uthey rob bhairab taney
	26	Eso shyamala sundara.	*Tamala* kunjapathey sajala chhayate
	31	Shanwana gaganey ghora ghanaghata	Shal-piyale tala *Tamaley* nibida timiramoy kunja
	35	Kanpichhe dehalata tharotharo	Dodul *Tamaleri* bana-chhaya
	39	Timira abagunthane	*Tamala*bana marmari
	62	Utal dhara badal jharey,	*Tamal*boney andhar karey, (3)
	74	Aji hriday amar jay je bhesey	Rajar purey *tamal* gachhe

Part	*Song number*	*Original song*	*Relevant line*
Prakriti	106	Ami shrabana akashey oi	Shyamala *Tamala* boney
	116	Trishnara shanti, sundara kanti,	*Tamala* bana shikhare naba-neela-anjana
	122	Mono mor meghera sangee,	Mono mor dhay tari matta prabahey tala *Tamala* aranye
	125	Ogo saontali chheley	Jhadey chanchala *Tamala* bonera praney
	132	Shesh ganeri resh niye jao choley,	*Tamala*-aranye oi shuni shesh keka
Bichitra	57	Se kon boner harin	*Tamala*-chhaye-chhaye
	75	Krishnakoli ami tarei boli,	Ashad masey name *tamal* boney
	139	(ami) Shrabana akashey oi	Shyamala *Tamala* boney
Prem O Prakriti	98	Barey barey phirey phirey	Talee *Tamalee* bonoraji neela

TAL, TALEE

(PALMYRA PALM)

"Mono mor dhay tari matta prabahe
tala tamala aranye"

Wild and frenzied movement (of the cloud) takes my mind hurridly to the groves of Tala (palmyra palm) and Tamala (egg-tree).

A tall, erect, branchless tree with round, dark green trunk bearing a terminal crown of many large, fan-shaped, bluish-green leaves, keeps its head high gazing at the sky. It draws exclusive attention of onlookers for its tallness and an erect, unbranched habit even when growing singly amidst a number of branched trees. Its structure helps it to swing merrily in a delirious mood making a low continuous sound when hit by the wind, which reminds performance of a gay dancing girl in a natural background.

The tree attains a height of 20-30 m with a trunk thickness of about 60 cm. Its leaves are as long as broad on short, stout, fibrous leaf-stalks. In a cluster at the apex, there may be 30-40 leaves about 1 m long. Male and female flowers are borne on separate plants. Inflorescence, large with many greenish-white flowers are covered with boat- shaped bracts known as spathes. Sex determination is difficult before flowering which may occur in

10-15 years. Male flowers are small, many and appear in clusters,while female flowers are fewer and scattered. Flowering is observed during spring (March-April). The fruits are oval or spherical and may ripen in 8-12 months. Each fruit has 3 nuts having soft, fleshy, white edible parts.

The tree is sacred to the Hindus and Buddhists. In ancient times, palm leaves were used for sacred scriptures. It is known that the 'Linga' or emblem of Lord Shiva in Tarakeshwar temple of West Bengal is made up of stumps of Palmyra Palm. (Sinha, R.P.N. – Our Trees, Palmyra Palm, Publication Division, Ministry of Information and Broadcasting, Government. of India, pp. 35, 1993). It is one of the most useful trees in India. Almost every part of it has specific economic and commercial use. In rural areas stems are used for roofing, leaves for thatching and making country umbrellas and fans; young fruits are refreshing. The inflorescence axis on being tapped exudes a sugary sap. Unfermented sap 'Neera' and fermented sap 'Toddy' are much in use. In short, every part of the tree is useful to people. It is propagated by seeds.

Not only in Tagore lyrics, but in other Indian classical literatures, these two plants — Tal and Tamal though dissimilar in several aspects, have been used in combination through the ages probably due to their lyrical and rhythmic proximity, close relationship with rains and for having dark-coloured stems. The plant originates from India and Malay regions and found in abundance in West Bengal, Bihar and along coastal regions of India, in gardens, in landscaping and in the open.

Part	*Song number*	*Original song*	*Relevant line*
Pooja	24	Ganer surer asankhani	*Taler* boney mather sheshey
Prem	181	Marana rey, tunhu mama	Shala*tala* taru sabhaya-tabadha saba
Prakriti	4	Aj taler boner karatali	Aj *Taler* boner karatali
	31	Shanwana gaganey ghora ghanaghata,	Shala-Piyale-*Tala*-Tamaley

Part	*Song number*	*Original song*	*Relevant line*
Prakriti	42	Ashadh, kotha hotey aj peli chhada	Nacher nesha laglo *Taler* patay patay
	60	Ei shrabaner buker bhitar	Kalo abhar kanpan dekho *Talboner* oi gachhe gachhe
	67	Ei sakalbelar badal-andharey	*Taler* pata mukhar korey toley rey
	107	Bhor theke aj badal chhutechhe	Ekakar holo teere ar neere *Tal*-talay
	122	Mono mor meghera sangee,	Mono mor dhay tari matta prabahey, *Tala*-Tamala aranye
	142	Megher koley rod hesechhe,	*Tal*dighitey bhashiye debo
	150	Ogo shephali bonera monera kamana,	Namo *Tala* pallaba beejaney
Prem O Prakriti	92	Barey barey phirey phirey	*Talee*-tamalee banaraji neela

DOORBA

(DOOB GRASS, BERMUDA GRASS)

"Nabashyam doorbadale
aloker jhalak jhale
paraner pulak bege"

The dazzle reflected over the dusty, bottle-green, new-born leafy mass of doorba (doob grass) exhibits an outburst of the joy of life.

Doorba, the green grass is an emblem of life, a symbol of freshness, longevity, vitality and eternity. It has the power to regenerate and retain its identity even under extremely adverse conditions teaching us the passion and urge to survive. In ancient Sanskrit literature, several citations of "doob" are found. Bluish-green colour of newly emerged leaves symbolizes the colour of Lord Rama and Lord Krishna in Hindu mythology. The Hindus consider it as an auspicious article and bless the youngsters with this grass and paddy-grains on religious or ceremonial occasions. It is a hardy perennial grass of creeping habit, spreading uniformly over the surface soil and rooting from stems at frequent intervals. It is widely grown in the plains of India and up to an elevation of 2000 m. The plant is rejuvenated during monsoon with bright colour. The leaves are smooth and narrow.

Its flowers white with red or violet tints are seen almost throughout the year.
In lyrics doorba is mentioned only twice but in many other song compositions, green grass in general (ghas, trina etc), are used. Although such grasses bear separate botanical identities, their appeal to people and nature is mostly alike.
Doob is one of the choicest grasses for lawn making for its look and is considered as a good fodder and soil binder. It is propagated by seeds and divisions.

Part	*Song number*	*Original song*	*Relevant line*
Prakriti	102	Dharanee, doorey cheye keno aj	Nabashyam *doorba*dale aloker jhalak jhaley paraner pulok begey
		TRINA, GHAS (GREEN GRASS)	
Pooja	17	Tomar kachhe e bar magi	Sethay *taru trina* jato
	26	Ganer bhitor diye jakhan dekhi bhubankhani	Takhan amar hriday kanpe tari *ghasey ghasey*
	53	Oder sathe melao	Kar ishara *triner* anguli
	355	Sarajeeban dilo alo	*Trina je* ei dhular parey patey anchalkhani
	520	Ei to tomar alokdhenu	*Triner* sari tulchhe matha
Prem	12	Nidrahara rater e gan bandhbo ami kemon surey	Nam-na-jana *trina kusum* shiurechhilo shishir jaley
	18	Ei kathati mone rekho	Shukno *ghasey* shoonyo boney apan mone
	23	Chhutir bnashi bajlo	Kanna abhas dey mele oi *ghasey ghasey*

Part	*Song number*	*Original song*	*Relevant line*
Prem	31	Amar paran loye	E nahe go *trinadal*
	77	Chapal taba nabeen ankhi duti	*Ghaser* chhoan nibhrita taruchhaye
	140	Se asey dheerey	Pushpita *trinabeethi*, jhankrita banageeti
	168	Kandar samay alpa orey	Kanna tader roilo podey sheerna *triner* koley
	169	Keno re etoi jabar twara	Taptadiner shushka *triner* asan meley
	194	Ogo amar chira-achena paradeshee	Chhilo podey *trinataley* ashokboney
	195	Kotha hotey shuntey jeno pai	Patay patay *ghasey ghasey* jegey othey deergha shwasey
	276	E pathey ami-jey	Uthilo boner *trina*
	295	O dekha diye jey chaley gelo	Beenar dhwani *triner* daley
	298	Gahana ghana boney	Sandhyabaye *trina*shayaney
	322	Elem natun deshey	Bajbey noopur boner *ghasey*
Prakriti	8	Akashbhara soorjo tara viswabhara pran	*Ghase ghase* pa phelechhi boner pathey jetey
	54	Kon puratan praner taney	Chokh dube jay nabeen *ghasey*
	64	Kakhan badal chhoan legey	Oi *ghaser* ghana ghorey
	69	Aji barsha rater sheshey	Ei *ghaser* jhilimili
	76	Brishtishesher haoa kiser khonje	Chinha padey boner *ghasey ghasey*
	98	Abar esechhe ashadh	Naba *trinadaley* badaler chhaya padey
	106	Ami shrabana akashey oi	Bedana jadaye achhe tari *ghasey*

Part	*Song number*	*Original song*	*Relevant line*
Prakriti	133	Esechhile tabu aso nai janaye geley	Chanchala charan gelo *ghasey ghasey* bedona meley
	146	Amar nayan-bhulano eley	Shishirbheja *ghase ghase* arunranga charan pheley
	156	Akash hotey khoslo tara	*Triney triney* shishir dhara
	158	Sara nishi chhilem shuey	Ejey *ghaser* koley alor bhasha
	185	Sheeter boney kon se kathin	Soyibena se patay *ghasey* pandurata
	206	Mor beena othey kon surey baji	Kar padaparashana asha *triney triney* arpilo bhasha
	233	Charana rekha tabo	Tarey jey *trinataley* ajikey leen dekhi
	238	Bakulgandhey banya elo dakhin haoar srotey	Patay patay *ghasey ghasey* nabeen praner patra asey
Bichitra	13	Jakhan podbey na mor payer chinha	Phuler bagan *ghana ghaser* porbey sajja banobaser
	77	Aaj taray taray	Hetha *ghasey ghasey* rongeen phuler alimpan
	93	Adhek ghumey nayan chumey	*Trina-anchal* petey
Natyageeti	21	Tarutaley chhinna-brinta malateer phul	Shushka *trinarashi* majhey ekela padia
Pooja O Prarthana	13	Prabhu elem kothay	Bhasiye kalsrotey *triner* pray
Anusthanic sangeet	16	Oi mahamanab asey	Martadhulir *ghasey ghasey*
Prem O Prakriti	61	Bujhi elo bujhi elo	*Ghasey ghasey* khabor chhotey
	76	Charan rekha tabo jey pathey dile lekhi	Tarey jey *trinataley* ajikey leen dekhi
	82	Ay tora ay ay go	Shishirkana *ghasey ghasey* shukiye asey

DOLONCHANPA

(GINGER LILY, BUTTERFLY LILY)

Popularly known as Dolonchanpa, this perennial, herbaceous, ornamental bulbous flowering plant is native of South-East Asia and grown in moist regions of India up to an elevation of 2000 m. Dolonchanpa has been used in Tagore's lyric only once in which the excellent floral quality of the plant has been revealed.

The plant attains a height of about 30-40 cm. Its rhizomes (underground modified stem) are flat and ginger-like, 2-5 cm thick. Dolonchanpa leaves are simple, large with long clasping sheaths. Inflorescence large, straight, branched — spike or raceme, surrounded by bracts which unfold slowly during emergence of floral axis. At the tip of the peduncle white, fragrant, showy, bisexual flowers appear in clusters. Sepals and petals are not much differentiated and are termed as perianth — floral tube 4-6 cm. Fragrance is more during evening. Blooming occurs mostly from the rains to autumn. When flowering its growth starts declining and leaves turn yellow.

The plant requires a partially shaded moist soil and not disturbed by water-logging for its growth and development. It has a number of economic and medicinal value. It is propagated by rhizomes.

Part	*Song number*	*Original song*	*Relevant line*
Prakriti	194	Doley doley	Doley premer *dolonchanpa*

DHAN, AUSH

(RICE)

"Hay hemantalakshmee, tomar nayan keno dhaka-
* * *
dharar anchal bhorey diley prachur sonar dhaney.
Diganganar angan aj poorna tomar daney."

Graceful 'Hemanta' (late autumn), adored as goddess of wealth and prosperity, why are your eyes veiled ... You have filled the vast expanse of the earth surface with plenty of golden paddy-grain making it full to the fullest measure with your precious gift.

The civilization, culture, meditation and livelihood of people of any region of the world are inseparably connected with plants. Civilization actually began with initiation of cultivation of crop. During the Vedic age agriculture was the major occupation of Indian people and rice with some other crop formed favourable commodities of food. Rice cultivation, however, took the lead and enforced confidence, peace and prosperity to the people through the ages. It has, therefore, been an integral part of economic, social, cultural, religious and literary aspects of the people. To many Indians it has become a symbol of affluence, prosperity and eternity. Blessing youngsters with paddy grain and doob grass reflects goodwill for their prosperity and longevity.

It is a grassy herbaceous annual growing all over India as a major crop. Its centre of origin is known to be in South-Eastern Asia with wide availability in India, Bangladesh, China, Myanmar and Thailand in regions getting adequate rainfall. The plant has fibrous roots. The stem is (culm) round, hollow and jointed with series of nodes and internodes. Its side shoots (tillers) are produced from the basal nodes on the main stem. Leaves consist of a flat leafblade and basal leaf sheath wrapping the stem. Flowers in panicles and spikelets form the grain.

As the crop is so much dependent on monsoon, the season is so dear to farmers. Seeds are sown soon after the early rains. At 3-4 leaved stages seedlings are raised from seed beds and transplanted in rain-fed or well-irrigated field. Flowers initially greenish white turn to yellow or golden yellow colour on maturity during autumn. The corp is harvested and stored afterwards. The early type or 'Aush' covers a period from April to September as against June to December by the other variety known as 'Aman'. 'Aush' has a special mention in one of the lyrical compositions – *"Neel nabaghaney ashadh gaganey"* (*Prakriti*, p. 108).

Apart from food, the straw and husk obtained from the crop have various domestic, ornamental and economic utility.

Part	*Song number*	*Original song*	*Relevant line*
Pooja	229	Tomar sonar thalai	Dhana *dhanya* tomari dhan
Swadesh	1	Amar sonar Bangla	Tomar *dhaney* bhara anginate
Prem	132	Aj sabar rongey rong mishatey hobey	Kancha sabuj *dhaner* kshetey
	159	Mukhopaney cheye dekhi	*Dhaney* bhara toree khani
Prakriti	72	Badal-baul bajay rey	Jamer boney *dhaner* kshetey
	96	Chaley chhalo chhalo nadeedhara	Oi jey uthe nabeen *dhanya* pulaki
	108	Neel nabaghaney ashadh gaganey	*Ausher* kshet jaley bharo-bharo

Part	*Song number*	*Original song*	*Relevant line*
Prakriti	125	Ogo saontali chheley	*Dhanera* ksheter parey
	126	Badala-dinera prathama kadama phul	Ksheter pratham sonar *dhan*
	143	Aj dhaner kshetey	Aj *dhaner* kshetey raudra chhayay
	144	Amra bendhechhi kasher guchchha	Nabeena *dhanera* manjaree diye
	152	Tomar mohana roopey	Paka *dhaner* taras lagey
	155	Kon kshyapa shraban chhute elo	Kiser kandan uthechhey aj nabeen *dhaney*
	167	Alor amala kamalakhani	Kochi *dhaner* sabuj kshetey
	172	Hay hemanta-lakshmee	Dharar anchal bhorey diley prachur sonar *dhaney*
	179	Poush toder dak diyechhe	i) Digbadhura *dhaner* kshetey ii) *Dhaner* shishey shishir legey
Bichitra	75	Krishnakali ami tarei boli	*Dhaner* kshetey kheliye gelo dheu
	130	Amra chash kori anandey	*Dhaner* shishey pulak chhotey
Anusthanik	16	Ay rey mora phasal kati	Mora nebo tari dan, tai jey kati *dhan*
Prem O Prakriti	64	Jaley doba chikan shyamal	Kochi *dhaner* pashey pashey

DHUTRO

(THORN APPLE)

"Ami chai tanre
amarey dilen jini sebikar samman,
jhorey pada dhutro phul
dhulo hotey tuley nilen jini dakshin karey"

I admire him who honoured me by accepting my service, as if with his right hand he picked up from the dust a fallen flower of thorn apple.

Dhutro is a shrub that grows wild in forests, waysides, wastelands and away from public view, uncared and unattended. Very often it blooms in its own style without least efforts to draw public attention and admiration, even though, it helps people immensely in a number of ways. It simply grows, develops and declines unlamented. Its sad and pitiable condition has been cited in Tagore's dance-drama *Chandalika*, which narrates the feelings and emotions of a lower caste woman considered untouchable by the dominant upper class society.

The plant is botanically known as *Datura stramonium*. It is an annual and a native of Asia reaching a height of 1-1.5 m. Its leaves are triangular, ovate and toothed with large flowers, white or pale violet, funnel-shaped that bloom during summer and the rains. Its leaves and seeds are narcotic, poisonous and intoxicating. Several parts of the plant are used in medicine. The plant is favourite to Lord Shiva, also known as Neelkantha, the blue-necked god who prefers a secluded abode not liked by many others.The flowers and fruits of this plant are offered to the Lord by the Hindu devotees on a special day of a Bengali year. It is propagated by seeds.

NAGKESHAR

(IRON-WOOD TREE)

Nagkeshar is a large, evergreen tree of pyramidal shape—native of Indo-Malayan region and distributed in West Bengal, Assam, Andamans, Western ghats and Eastern Himalayas. The tree attains a height up to 15 m with spreading base, bark greyish or reddish brown.The wood is very hard and durable. Its leaves are long, narrow, arranged in opposite pairs, red at early stages turning to green later. The flower is large, white, deliciously scented with numerous yellow, thread-like stamens at the centre forming a golden ball, which are shed after getting dried up. Flowering occurs from late winter to summer in profusion. The fruits are egg-shaped.

In a letter from abroad, Tagore expresses his love for this plant: "How often I had thought I would witness the manifestation of a limitless motion in the flowers of the nagkeshar. They echo the music of the hymns of meditation of the universe". (Ghosh, P.K. *et al. Tagore and Flowers,* Publication and Information Directorate, New Delhi 92, 1993). He has used this plant only once in his lyric, but in his poems, there are many references. Besides serving as an ornamental flowering specimen of the garden, its flowers and flower buds are used in cosmetics. Other parts, viz. seeds, woods and fruits have various domestic, economic and medicinal uses. The plant is propagated by seeds.

Part	*Song number*	*Original song*	*Relevant line*
Prem	173	Keno amay pagol korey jas	Nag*kesharer* jhara keshar dhular sathey mita

NARIKEL

(COCONUT TREE)

"Coconut trees grow easily in areas along sea coasts. Our 'ashrama' land is far away from the sea coast. A sapling of coconut has been raised here with great care – it is solitary, barren and lacking vitality. In this non saline soil, there is no impact of the sea; the root seeks desired nutrients but is not getting the same. It is hungry, its tearful appeal fails to get any sympathetic response from the land."

The coconut tree is held in high esteem in India and is believed as a symbol of life and abundance. The fruits green or dry, are considered very auspicious and sacred to the Hindus and used in their religious and ceremonial occasions.

It is a tall, erect, unbranched tree with more or less crooked trunk (10-20 m) bearing a crown of feather-like, large, green leaves. Its origin is questionable, may be a native of islands off the Pacific coasts of Panama or South or Central America and has been in cultivation along the sea-coasts and in the saline tracts of several regions of the world.

The trunk bears a number of semicircular scars indicating locations of fallen leaves.The leaf is 2-4 m long, leaflets are about 1 m, sword-shaped and arranged on either side of the midrib-petiole about 1-1.5 m, stout and channelled, and the base is wrapped with cover of coarse and strong fibres. The plant bears both male and female flowers on the same individual. The flower stalk (1-2 m) is initially covered by a boat-shaped bract (spathe), about 1 m in length which ultimately splits lengthwise revealing the inflorescence (spadix). The female flowers are few at the base, larger than the male flowers at the apex which are sweet scented. The flowers form mature fruits in 9-10 months. The fruit, known as coconut, is covered with tough and fibrous husks.

The tree may start bearing in 5-7 years along sea-coasts and saline tracts under favourable conditions. But in unfavourable locations, bearing may be delayed up to 25 years.

It is a plant of great aesthetic and commercial value besides its use in ornamental and landscape gardening. Green coconuts serve as a refreshing drink—toddy is extracted from the flowering spikes and the leaves are used for thatching, the fibre (coir) is used for making ropes, carpets, mattresses, etc. and oil extracted from raw kernel is a good cooking medium. The plant is propagated by seeds.

Tagore in his lyric, has used this plant only once. The branches as referred to in the composition, probably indicate the feather-like leaves with stout axis as the plant is unbranched.

Part	*Song number*	*Original song*	*Relevant line*
Bichitra	99	Jaboi ami jaboi ogo	*Narikeler* shakhey shakhey

NEELSHATADAL, NEELPADMA, NEELAMBUJ
(BLUE LOTUS)

Neelshatadal or blue lotus has its reference in the Ramayana, one of the great epics of the Hindus. It has been sanctified by the Aryans as a symbol of Lord Vishnu – a symbol of stability and eternity. However, lots of confusion lies in this name. The origin, character and availability of Neelpadma, as mentioned in the epic, need exhaustive study. It is still believed in some quarters that the plant was available in the Manas Sarovar of Kailash (Tibet) but the climatic condition and location of this place is not at all congenial to the growth of any aquatic flora. According to Havel (*Indian Sculpture and Painting*), the flower in the hand of Tara, the sacred idol of the Buddhists, was none other than the blue lotus. Such ancient references on the plant may give rise to two sets of thinking—either it was simply a wishful expression of the mind or the species has been lost through the ages as a result of poor conservation.

The flowers, known as Neelpadma in India, are stirctly waterlilies and not lotuses. Though these two plants belong to different families, they have various things in common. Both are perennial, rhizomatous, aquatic, ornamental, herbaceous, flowering plants with leaves floating on water and flowers visible almost throughout the year, mostly after the rainy season till fall of winter. Waterlilies have, however, less number of petals than lotuses. Both the plants are commonly propagated by division of rhizomes or tubers.

Indian blue waterlily (*Nymphaea stellata*), a native of South-East Asia and Egyptian blue lotus (*Nymphaea caerulea*), a native of Africa—two blue flowering waterlilies—as have been recorded in India since ancient times, are now grouped in one species viz., *Nymphaea nouchali* because of their close morphological characters. The leaves are 12-20 cm, orbicular or elliptical, the upper surface is green, and the lower surface bluish-purple with blue, bluish or bluish-purple flowers.

At present a number of exotic species and varieties of waterlilies are cultivated in gardens of India exhibiting blue, bluish-purple and violet colours. Some of these are: *Nymphaea capensis* (cape blue waterlily), *Nymphaea elegans, Nymphaea micrantha, Nymphaea x daubeniana, Nymphaea gigantea, Nymphaea pulcherrima, Nymphaea zanzibariensis* and the varieties are: 'August Koch', 'Blue Beauty', 'Blue Triumph', 'Carls Brookii', 'Col. Lindberg', 'Col. Louis Emerson', 'Director George T. Moore', 'King of Blues', 'Margaret Randig', "Mrs. Edward Whitaker', 'Mrs. Martin E. Randig', 'Panama Pacific', 'Pamela' and 'Pennsylvania'. These were however, not prevalent in India at a time when Tagore composed the lyric. Thus it appears that Tagore's Neelpadma or Neelshatadal specify the traditional Nymphaea nouchali. It is propagated by seeds and rhizomes.

Part	*Song number*	*Original song*	*Relevant line*
Pooja	304	Kee gabo ami,	Aseem akash *neelshatadal*
	546	Ami kan petey roi	Bhramar setha hoy bibagi nibhrita *neelpadma* lagi rey
Prakriti	1	Biswabeenarabey biswajan mohichhe	Oti nirmala hasa bibhasabikasha akasha *neelambuja* majhey

PADMA, SHATADAL, NALINEE, KAMAL
(LOTUS)

A popular aquatic herb, Padma is a native of China, Japan and probably India. It grows on the surface of fresh water ponds and lakes. It is a sacred flower to the Hindus and Buddhists and has been in cultivation in India since the time of the great epics. In the Ramayana, mentions are made of palace gardens which had "numerous birds and flowers, shady groves of fruit trees and lakes with lotuses." (Randhawa, M.S., *Gardens Through the Ages*, 1976). It has been recorded that Siddhartha (Lord Buddha) saw flowering trees and lotuses in Nandanvan. In ancient literature, mention has been made of three kinds of Padma – Shwetpadma or White lotus (Pundareeka), Raktapadma or Red lotus (Kokonada) and Neelpadma or Blue lotus (Indeebar). Confusion still exists on nomenclature of *Neelpadma* and majority are of opinion that blue lotus or neelpadma is actually the blue waterlily. References of padma are also found in the Vedas and Kalidasa's plays Meghdoota and Shakuntala.

The herb (padma) so dear to us, is a perennial rhizomatous, ornamental water plant. The roots and rhizomes stick to the mud, rhizomes stout and creeping. Its leaves are large, round, smooth with a cylindrical stalk attached to the centre, dark green on upper side, somewhat pale beneath, raised above water when young and floating when old. The flower is large, showy, solitary,

white, rose, pink or amaranth red, somewhat fragrant—petals about 20 in single form and more than 100 in double form, free. Flowering occurs during summer and monsoon, opening at day time and closing with the onset of darkness. The fruit is spongy with many cavities for seeds and resemble the rose of a watering can. The plant increases by seeds and rhizomes.
Besides beautifying the environment, the flower has its use in various social and religious purposes as cut flowers and loose flowers. The rhizomes and seeds are edible.
In lyrics, the plant is mentioned 101 times covering various aspects of its morphological, social, religious and human appeal.

Part	*Song number*	*Original song*	*Relevant line*
Pooja	6	Tumi jey surer agun	Uthlo phutey *swarnakamal*
	7	Tomar beena amar manomajhey	Chalitechhinu tabo *kamal*-boney
	125	Padaprantey rakho sebakey	Bikasitadala *chittakamala*
	137	Jey din phutlo kamal kichhui jani nai	Je din phutlo *kamal*
	152	Lakshmee jakhan asbey	Dyakhrey cheye apan-paney *padmati* nai
	177	Pratidin tabo gatha	Bikacha *kama-lasaney*
	188	E abaran kshoy hobey	Biswa*kamal* praney amar
	199	Ami marer sagar	Amar duksha diner *raktakamal*
	207	Mor maraney tomar hobey joy	Mor duksha jey ranga *shatadal*
	213	Ke rey eman jagay tokey ?	*Raktashatadaler* saji
	240	Ananda tumi swami, mangala tumi	Shubhra shanti *shatadal* punya madhupaney
	247	Har-mana har	*Shatadaladal* khuley jabe tharey tharey

Part	*Song number*	*Original song*	*Relevant line*
Pooja	251	Aji kon dhan hotey	Taba *charan-kamal-* ratan renuka
	264	Shuvra naba sankha taba	Mama *hriday-kamala* bikashita
	271	Nishar swapan chhutla re,	Hriday *shatadaler* sakal dalguli
	272	Anek diner shoonyata mor	Milan *shatadaley* tomar premer arup murti dekhao bhubantaley
	278	Manomohana, gahana jaminee-sheshey	Shanti sarasee majhey chitta *kamala*
	316	Premey praney ganey	*Shatadalasama* phutilo param harashey
	321	Bajey bajey ramya beena	Amala *kamala* majhey
	325	Amala kamala sahajey jalera koley	Amala *kamala* sahajey jalera koley anandey rahey phutia
	328	Heri tabo bimala-mukhabhati	Dinu hridaya *kamaladala* pati
	359	Nitya tomar je phul photey	*Bishwakamal* phutey charan chumbaney
	360	Emani korey ghuriba doorey bahirey	Tomar chhaya pade jey sarobarey go, *kamal* setha dharey na, nahi dharey go
	406	Himsay unmatta prithbee	Bikashita karo *premapadma*
	428	Kar milana chao birahee	Chitta *kamaley* charanpadma rajey
	454	Banchan banchi maren mari	Hridaya *padmadaley* charan aloy dhanya kari

Part	*Song number*	*Original song*	*Relevant line*
Pooja	461	Eki karuna karunamoya !	Hridaya *shatadal* uthila phuti amala kiraney tabo padataley
	462	Peyechhi sandhan tabo antarjamee	Hriday *shatadala* majhey
	492	Amar matha nata korey	Amarey adal koria dandao hridaya-*padmadaley*
	503	Nomi nomi charaney	Nomi *chittakamala-daley*
	505	Tomari namey nayan melinu	Tomari namey khulilo hridaya *shatadala* dala raji
Prem	7	Ganer dali bhorey de go	*Kamalbaran* gagan-majhey *kamalcharan* oi birajey
	29	Bajila kahara beena	Pravata*kamala*samo phutilo hridaya mamo
	33	Amarey karo tomar beena	Komal tabo *kamal* karey
	48	Amar nayan tabo nayaner nibid chhayay	Duarey enkechhi raktarekhay *padma-asan*
	50	Aro kichhukshan na hoy bosio pashey	*Raktakamal* tarangey talo-molo
	88	Aha, tomar sangey praner khela	Ei *hritkamaler* ranga renu
	181	Marana rey, tunhun mama	*Raktakamal* kar
	187	Ohey sundara, mama grihey aji	Rekhechhi kanaka-mandirey *kamalasana* pati
	215	Gopana kathati	Hridaya *shatadala*
	239	Bhara thak smriti sudhay	Paraner *padma* boney biraher beenapani
	261	Na chahiley jarey paoa jay	Beenabadineer *shatadaladaley*

Part	*Song number*	*Original song*	*Relevant line*
Prem	265	Nai jodi ba eley tumi	*Milankamal* uthechhe duley
	284	Ekla bosey ekey ekey	*Padmer* dal bhasao jaley akaraney
	375	Jaubanasarasee neerey	Milana-*shatadala*
Prakriti	144	Amra bendhechhi kasher guchchha	Mukutey paria *shwetshatadala*
	149	Aj pratham phuler pabo prasadkhani	Hiran-kiran-*padmadaley*
	151	Sharata-alor kamalaboney	Sharata-alor *kamalaboney*
	167	Alor amala kamalakhani	Alor amala *kamalakhani*
	189	Eso eso basanta, dharataley	Aruncharan *kamal*-baran
	223	O chand, tomay dola	Kon madhureer *kamal*kanan
	267	Orey bakul, parul,	Akool abakashe jethay swapna *kamal* bhasey
	272	Aji kamala mukula dal	Aji *kamala*-mukula dal khulila
Bichitra	2	Nrityera taley taley	Amala*kamala* gandha hey
	8	Kamalaboner madhuparaji	*Kamala*boner madhuparaji
	10	Madhura madhura dhwani bajey	Hridaya*kamala*-bana-majhey
	20	Hater dhula soy na jey ar	Tomar ganer *padmaboney*
	91	Tumi ushara sonara bindu	Amala alor *kamalaboney*
	112	Amra lakshmee-chhadar dal	Bhaber *padma*-patrey jal
	131	Tomra hasiya bohiya chalia jao	*Kamalcharan* porhichhe dharanee-majhey
Natyageeti	7	Nach, shyama, taley taley,	*Kamalakarer* karatali heno

Part	*Song number*	*Original song*	*Relevant line*
Prem O Prakriti	6	Golap phul phutiye achhe	Hothay achhe *nalinee* —
	9	Shuna nalinee, kholo go ankhi —	Shun *nalinee* kholo go ankhi
	50	Jeebaney e ki pratham basanta elo	*Shatadala* dal meliyachhe amar mon
	57	Bidhi dagar ankhi	Duti atul *padatal* ratul *shatadal*
	63	Tarun prater arun akash	Akool-manas-sagar-jaley *kamal* talomalo
Prakriti	267	Orey bakul parul, Orey shalpiyaler bon	Jethay swapna-*kamal* bhasey
Prem O Prakriti	84	Jhankda chuler meyer katha	Nam chhilo tar *swarnanalinee*

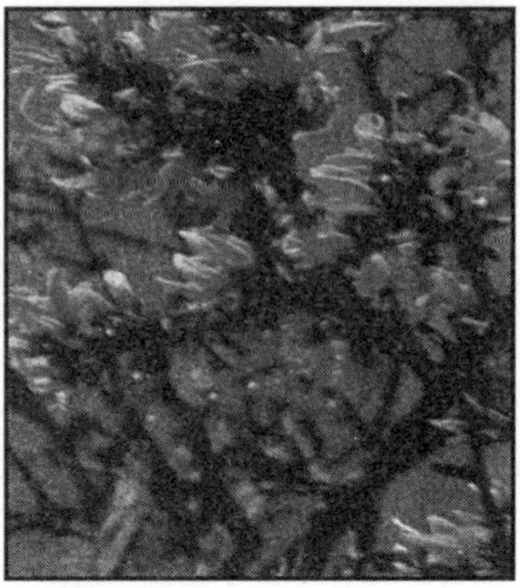

PALASH, KIMSHUK
(PARROT TREE, FLAME OF THE FOREST)

"Je basante utkanthita dine
sarha elo chanchal dakshine;
palasher kundi
ek ratre barnabanhi jwalilo
samasta bon judi;"

Restless southern wind is enlivened on arrival of the eagerly awaited spring. In one single night the entire forest is dazzled by the profuse blooms of palasha buds in clusters.

It is one of the important, native ornamental flowering trees of India, sacred to the Hindus and frequently mentioned in the ancient literatures. Three leaflets of its leaf are believed to be symbolical representations of Brahma, Vishnu and Shiva. According to Kalidasa, the great poet of ancient India, the earth looks like a bride in red marital dress when a fully bloomed *Palash* forest starts bearing orange-red flowers in spring. The tree was also a favourite to Tagore for its majestic display of crimson-scarlet flowers overflowing with beauty, youth and vitality and also for being a forerunner of spring.
It is a small or medium-sized (7-12 m) deciduous tree with crooked trunk and irregular, twisted branches. Its leaves are large and

trifoliate, leaflets almost ovate. In winter, the tree becomes almost leafless followed by transformation into a genuine flame by appearance of clusters of attractive, deep-scarlet, orange-red or crimson-scarlet non-odorous flowers, which signifies its name – 'Flame of the forest'. Among the five petals the bottom one looks like a parrot's beak for which the tree is also known as parrot tree or Kimshuk in Sanskrit, meaning – 'Is it a parrot'? Blooming starts with the advent of spring and continues up to summer. New leaves appear after flowering, followed by fruit setting. It is propagated by seeds.

The tree is a witness to several historical and religious events. It is believed by a section of the Buddhists that Gautama Buddha was born under the shade of this tree. The battle of Plassey was fought in a place where several *Palash* trees formed a forest-like look. The twigs are offered in *homa* along with *ghee* (clarified butter) to the sacred fire. 'Bengal Kino' a gum is exuded from the stem. Palash flowers yield a vegetable dye which is used in rural areas during colour festivals (Holi). In Santiniketan, chains and garlands of *Palasha* flowers are often used during *Vasantotsav* (Spring festival) or 'Holi' (Colour festival). Fascinating and appealing colour of flowers mainly find expression in Tagore's lyrics.

Part	*Song number*	*Original song*	*Relevant line*
Prem	45	He sakha, barata peyechhi	Dekha dao *kimshukey* kanchaney
	251	Rodanabhara e basanta,	Birhabedana rangalo *kimshuka* raktima ragey
	270	Ashanti aj hanlo	Phagundiner *palash* ronger rangin mayatey
Prakriti	184	Mora bhangba tapas,	*Palash* renur rong makhiey
	197	Orey grihabasee	Ranga hasi rashi rashi ashokey *palashey*
	198	Ektuku chhoan lagey,	Kichhu *palasher* nesha

Part	*Song number*	*Original song*	*Relevant line*
Prakriti	199	Ogo bodhoo sundaree,	*Palasher* kumkum
	205	Akash amay bharlo aloy,	Orey *palash,* orey *palash*
	235	Tomar asan patba kothay	*Palash* bakul byakul hobey atmadaney
	238	Bakulgandhey banya elo	*Palashkali* dikey dikey
	240	An go tora	*Palashkanan* dhairya haray ranger jhadey
	241	Phagun, haoay haoay	Tomar ashokey *kimshukey*
	245	Phagunera nabeena anandey	Banee mama nila tuli *palasher* koliguli
	271	Amar malar phuler daley,	*Kimshukshakha* chanchal holo
	282	Phagun-haoay rangey rangey	*Palash*-parijater buker parey
Bichitra	83	Je kebal paliye beday,	Aji ki *palash*boney oi se bulay ranger tuli

PARIJAT

(HOLY TREE)

Parijat is believed to be a holy tree of heaven bearing flowers of exquisite beauty and heavenly qualities. According to Hindu mythology, the tree came out from the ocean as a by-product following churning for getting nectar which would ensure immortality. It was then taken to the heavenly garden of Lord Indra at Amaravati. Lord Krishna stole the plant from the garden and brought it down to earth. This legend reveals the inherent quality of the tree and its flowers. But it is not clearly understood whether this *Parijat* is simply an imagination or a reality. The reason behind it lies in the facts that in modern time a number of flowers are mentioned as *Parijat.*

According to ancient Indian literature, Mandar and Parijat *are* identical. Shushruta, an ancient Indian exponent of medicine also favoured this view. In the two C.S.I.R. publications – "*Wealth of India* " (1948 – 1976) and '*The Useful Plants of India*' (1976)—the same view has been repeated. It is said that in the gardens of Amaravati, Mandar played a significant role in beautification. Botanically, the plant is known as *Erythrina variegata* or *orientalis*, a native of India and distributed in the deciduous forests. In English, it is the Indian coral tree, *Palte madar* or *Parijata* in Bengali. It is a medium-sized (7–12 m) deciduous tree with trifoliate, light-green leaves—the three leaflets are known to represent the three Hindu gods – Brahma, Vishnu and Maheshwara. Scarlet or deep red flowers in terminal clusters are found in early spring under completely defoliated condition. It is planted in parks and gardens and grown in rural areas to serve as live poles for fencing.

Scientists are unanimous on the botanical identity of Mandar but opinions differ in some quarters regarding Parijat. In *Tree planting Ceremony of Santiniketan* (1984), it is mentioned that in 1966, Surendranath Kar planted a sapling of Parijat (*Brownea grandiceps*) near Navanandan. This evergreen ornamental tree, popularly known as Rose of Venezuela, is a native of West Indies and bears beautiful reddish-purple flowers in semi-globose, drooping clusters from March to May. Numerous red stamens with tall filaments rise above the petals bearing light yellow pollens. In *Tagore and Flowers*, (1993), *Brownea ariza* of American origin, in some others *Erythrina crista-galli*, popularly known as Cockspur coral tree of Brazilian origin, has been referred to as Parijat. All the three species stated above bear beautiful but non-odorous flowers. In *Garden Flower*, (Swarup, V. 1991), *Nyctanthes arbor-tristis* (Shiuli in Bengali) has been mentioned as Parijat as per ancient Sanskrit literature. This tree, however, bears beautiful and exceedingly fragrant flowers blooming at night.

In lyrics on Parijat, there is more appreciation for its fragrance than colour. In "Prem", 94, the kesara (hair) probably refers to filaments of *Brownea grandiceps* and in "Prakriti" 282 *Parijat* has been shown in combination with Golap (Rose), Jaba (China rose), Parul (Trumpet flower) and Palash (Parrot tree) — all red flowering plants. Here the Mandar has been in view probably. All these may lead us to believe that Parijat as visualized by Tagore, is simply a poetic expression of his imagination of a beautiful flower of heaven, be it fragrant or not.

Part	*Song number*	*Original song*	*Relevant line*
Prem	94	Chander hasir bandh bhengechhe	*Parijater* keshar niye (With hairy stamens of parijat flowers)
	110	Amar praner majhey	*Parijater* madhur gandha (sweet smell of parijat flowers)
Prakriti	246	Bedana kee bhashay rey	*Parijatmala* sugandha haney
	282	Phagun-haoay rangey rangey	Palash *parijater* buker parey
Bichitra	71	Tomader dan jasher dalay	Genthechhinu mala jharey-pada *parijatey*
Natyageeti	113	Namo namo shachee chita ranjana	Tabo padapatey nabo *parijatey*

PARUL

(TRUMPET-FLOWER)

Parul is a tall deciduous tree, 15m or more in height and distributed in the drier parts of India, in forests and in some conservation centres of West Bengal, Bihar and Jharkhand. The tree is very intimately associated with Bengali folklore and folk stories since ancient times. In Sanskrit, it is known as Patalee, a name that sounds like Pataleeputra, now Patna of Bihar. Patalee might have derived from Patal indicating pale red or pink petals of its flowers. The tree becomes leafless in winter, and new leaves emerge in spring followed by flowers. The fascinating flower colour, its fragrance and a poetic name of the plant had made it so appealing to the people of ancient India.

The tree bears pinnately compound leaves (30 – 50cm) on long branches with 7 – 9 leaflets (10 – 15cm), elliptic–oblong with long and narrow apex, gradually tapering to the base. Parul flowers bloom in large panicles on a long floral stalk (40-60cm) in various shades of colour. The 'trumpet-flower' or '*Parul*', now botanically known as *Stereospermum colais* (synonym: S. s*uaveolens*, *S. personatum*), bears flowers as follows:

i) Flowers bright yellow, cream within with dark red stripes (*S. personatum*)

ii) Flowers pale or dark purple, deep violet, coppery brown with light violet stripes (*S. suaveolens*)

Trumpet or bell-shaped, small and somewhat scented flowers (3-4 cm), are visible at the onset of spring and continues up to summer. Flowers of S. personatum are comparatively smaller than those of S. suaveolens.
In ancient Sanskrit drama Shakuntala, there is mention of pleasing and delicately scented Parul flowers in summer days.

Part	*Song number*	*Original song*	*Relevant line*
Prem	105	Noopur beje jay	*Parul* shudhailo ke tumi go
Prakriti	149	Aj pratham phuler pabo prasadkhani,	Aj *Paruldidir* boney mora chalbo nimantraney
	199	Ogo badhoo sundaree.	*Paruler* hillol
	267	Orey Bakul, Parul,	Orey Bakul *Parul*
	275	Biday niye giyechhilem	Ke go tumi 'ami *parul*'
	282	Phagun-haoay rangey rangey	Golap jaba *Parul* Palash Parijater buker parey
Natyageeti	132	Kothao amar hariye jaoar	*Parul* boner champarey mor hoy jana
Prem O Prakriti	67	Orey Bakul *Parul,*	Orey Bakul *Parul,* orey shal piyaler bon

PIYAL

(CUDDAPAH ALMOND)

"There is a tree in Santiniketan
which according to some is Piyal.
But how many among us
are familiar with the famous
Piyal as mentioned in Sanskrit
literature"

But the tree could not escape attention of the poet's ever-inquisitive mind and his observation on the tree finds expression as follows:

Shudhu shoonya birat prantarbhoomi
tari prante nirala piyal taru tumi
* * * *
tomar manjaree
kabhu phote, kabhu padey jhari,
tomar pallabdal
kabhu stabdha, kabhu ba chanchal.

Piyal tree, you stand isolated at the outskirts of a vast barren compound...sometimes your floral spikes are in bloom, at times they drop down, sometimes the leaves are found calm and motionless while at times they are restless and oscillating.

Like shal, tal and tamal, piyal is also basically a forest tree, not in much use as an ornamental plant for garden beautification, but a fine rhythmical arrangement of these names in a group, makes them so fascinating and poetical that they appear frequently in lyrical compositions of poets and lyricists. The tree is distributed in the dry deciduous forests and in low rainfall regions of India and Myanmar.

Pial is a medium-sized tree (10-15m) with nearly one metre girth; thick dark-grey bark (2-2.5cm) having small quadrangular fissures. Its leaves are large (10-15cm), brownish, oblong, obtuse-undersurfaces slightly pubescent, petiole small (0.5 – 0.8 cm). Tiny greenish-white flowers (0.6 cm), in a branched inflorescence (panicle) like that of mango, appear at the onset of spring. In a flower, there are 10 stamens which bear yellow pollens on the tip of filaments as expressed in "*Prakriti*", 202. Fruiting occurs at the end of spring. The fruit is small (0.6 cm), black and almost round. Numerous drooping, black-coloured fruits on branches swing in the air like innumerable black hair as have been rightly expressed in the lyrics ("Prem" 102 and "Prakriti" 41). Seeds borne by the small fruits are edible and known as 'chiranjee' which is regarded and used as a substitute for almond. Medicinal value of its fruits and seeds were perhaps known in ancient India during the periods of Charaka and Shushruta. The plant is propagated by seeds.

Part	*Song number*	*Original song*	*Relevant line*
Prem	102	Achho akashpaney tuley matha	*Piyalboney* udalo chul
	256	Dhoosar jeebaner godhoolitey	Jei rong *piyal* chhayay dhaley shukla saptameer tithi
	298	Gahan ghana boney	*Piyal*-tamal-saha-kar-chhaye
Prakriti	1	Bishwabeena robey bishwajana mohichhe	*Piyal* tamal-bitaney uthey rob bhairaba-taney
	31	Shanwana gaganey ghora ghanaghata,	Shal-*piyaley* tal-tamaley

Part	*Song number*	*Original song*	*Relevant line*
Prakriti	41	Kadamberi kanan gheri	*Piyalguli* nater thatey haoay heley
	111	Oi malateelata doley	*Piyal* tarur koley
	193	Kar jena ei moner bedan	*Piyalboner* shakhay nachey
	202	Aji dakhina-duar khola	Eso bajaye byakula benu mekhey *Piyala* phulera renu
	260	Neel akasher koney koney	Shal-*piyaler* boney boney kemon jena knapan jagey
	267	*Orey Bakul, Parul,*	*Orey* shal-*piyaler* bon
Bichitra	57	Se kon boner harin	Phalguney se *Piyaltalay*
Prem O Prakriti	67	Orey Bakul Parul,	Orey shal-*piyaler* bon

BAKUL

(INDIAN MEDLAR, SPANISH CHERRY)

"Hriday amar nacherey ajikey
mayoorer mato nacherey
* * * *
ogo nirjaney Bokul shakhaye
dolaye ke aji dulichhey, dodul dulichhey.
Jharakey jharakey jharichhe Bokul,
anchal akashey hotechhey akul,
urhia alak dhakichhey palak
kabaree khasia khulichhey"

Today my soul dances in joy like a peacock, O' who swings there in solitude on Bakul branches. Flowers in profusion drop incessantly from the Bokul tree, the expanse of the end of worn cloth looking at the sky anxiously, dishevelled hair covering the vision and braid getting loose.

Bakul is a famous tree in Tagore's Santiniketan. In his lyrics, it has been mentioned 73 times in various ways like Bakul (the tree), Bakul-phul (the flowers), Bakul-bon (the grove), Bakul-beethi (the avenue), Bakul-tala (the base of the tree) and Bakul-bedee (an elevated masonry structure or altar at the tree base). The tree, a native of India, Myanmar and Sri Lanka, grows almost in every corner of India.

A medium-sized (10-15m), evergreen, ornamental flowering tree of pyramidal shape with straight trunk, spreading branches and dense crown of foliage. This quality of the tree makes it pleasing to walk and rest in the shade of its groves and avenues. Due to slow growth of the branches, the tree may be pruned in the shape of an umbrella which will persist for a longer period. The bark is rough and dark grey and the leaves are shiny, thick, narrow and pointed with upper surface deep green, undersurface pale green and margin wavy. Bakul flowers are small (1.5cm), star-shaped, fragrant, creamy-white to pale-green in colour, borne in clusters from March to July. They are shed at night and in the morning the tree bases are found covered with a large number of sweet-scented flowers which retain the smell even when dried up. Fruits are borne during summer and the rainy seasons. These are small, smooth, shiny, cherry-like green berries turning to red or vermilion when ripe.

Since ancient times the tree, its buds and flowers, have found place in literary works of poets and lyricists. Buds and flowers are excellent materials for making floral ornaments such as hairbands, garlands and ear-rings. Flowers yield *maulsari* essence. The tree is also grown in gardens, avenues, near temples and other religious places. It may live even for 80-100 years standing as a mute witness to the rise and fall of many political, social, cultural and religious events in a region. It is propagated by seeds.

Part	*Song number*	*Original song*	*Relevant line*
Pooja	28	Jatokhan tumi amay bosiye rakho	Phagun diner *Bakul* chanpa
Prem	11	Akashey aj kon charaner asa-jaoa	*Bakultalaye* kaj-bhola sei kon dupurey
	19	Asa-jaoar pather dharey	Kon chaitramasey *Bakul*-dhaka boner ghasey
	39	He nirupama,	*Bakul* beethika mukuley matta kanan-'porey
	56	Ogo shono ke bajay	*Bakulguli* akul hoye banshir ganey munjarey

Part	*Song number*	*Original song*	*Relevant line*
Prem	61	Sakhee, pratidin haye	Setha asan bichhaye rakhis *bakuldaley.*
	102	Achho, akashpaney tuley matha	Piyalboney udalo chul, *bakulboney* anchal pata
	108	Meghachhaye sajal baye	Kon basanter nisheethey jey sey *bakulmalakhani* paraley
	134	Amar dosar jey jan	Jakhan *bakul* jhorey amar kanantal jaye go bhorey
	138	Mamo jouban nikunjey	Jago nabeen gourabey, naba *bakul* souravey
	168	Kandar samay alpo orey,	Jabar diney shukno *bakul* mithye koris jado
	169	Keno rey etai jabar twara —	Bidayer pathey hatash *bakul*
	175	Klanta banshir shesh raginee	Pathik ami esechhilem tomar *bakultaley*
	185	O amar dhyaneri dhan,	Asey basanta, photey *bakul*
	186	Haye rey, orey jay na ki jana.	Jhorey-pada *bakuldaley* bichhaye bichhana
	188	Ke amarey jeno	*Bakul* jharia moribarey chaye kahar chuley
	216	Balo sakhee, balo	Sey nam madir hobey jey *bakul*ghraney
	218	Dhara sey jey deya nai,	Jharey-pada *bakuler* gandhe
	222	Ami tomar sangey	Se sadhanaye mishiya jaye *bakulgandha*
	230	Adhara madhuree	Tomari *bakulboner* ganeyo deye sada –
	259	Phirbey na ta jani,	Tabu dharuk mukul amar *bakulboney*

Part	*Song number*	*Original song*	*Relevant line*
Prem	268	Kon gahan aranye	*Bakultalaye* chhayar nachan
	298	Gahano ghana boney	*Bakuldal* pade khasi
	304	Kakhan jey basanta gelo,	Kakhan *bakulmool* chheyechhilo jhara phul
	305	Banshari bajatey chahi	Bikach *bakulphul* dekhey jey hotechhe bhul
	318	Doorer bandhu surer dooteerey	*Bakulshakhar* chanchalataye marmarey
	383	Bidaye korechha jarey	Tare ki padechhe money *bakultaley*
Prakriti	9	Byakul bakuler phuley	Byakul *bakuler* phuley
	19	Baishakher ei bhorer hawa	Adho ghumer pranto chhoan *bakulmalar* gandha
	26	Eso shyamal sundara,	*Bakulmukul* rekhechhi ganthia
	45	Shravanbarishana par hoye	Sikta *bakuler* banataley
	96	Chaley chhalo chhalo nadeedhara	Kooley prafulla *bakulbon*
	110	Aji pallibalika alakaguchchha sajalo	*Bakul* phuler duley,
	113	Hriday amar nachey rey	Nirjane *bakulsha-khaye* dolaye ke aji dulichhe
	147	Shiuliphul, shiuliphul	Daley daley jaye *bakul*
	173	Hemantey kon basanteri banee	*Bakul* daler agaye jyotsna jeno phuler swapan lagaye
	184	Mora bhangba tapas,	*Bakulboner* mugdha hridaye uthuk na uchchhasi
	191	Enechha oi shireesh bakul	Enechha oi shireesh *bakul*

Part	*Song number*	*Original song*	*Relevant line*
Prakriti	202	Aji dakhin-duar khola	Eso *bakulbichhano* pathey
	214	Baki ami rakhba na kichhui—	Ujad korey deba paye *bakul-bela-*juin
	221	(Oi) bhanglo hasir bandh	Mukul-chhaoa *bakulboney*
	226	Aj dakhin-batase	*Bakul* tomar malar majhey
	229	Na, jeo na,	Ajo *bakul* apanhara
	235	Tomar asan patbo kothaye	Palash *bakul* byakul hobey atmadaney
	238	Bakulgandhey banya elo	*Bakulgandhey* banya elo
	243	He madhabee, dwidha keno,	*Bakul* peyechhe chhada
	245	Phaguner nabeen anandey	Bhari dila *bakuler* gandhey
	247	Chaley jaye mori haye	Adheer sameer-bhore uchchhasi *bakul* jharey
	266	Ei phaguner gan sey amar	Shudhaye tarey *bakul* hena
	267	Orey bakul, parul,	Orey *bakul*, parul
	271	Amar malar phuler	*Bakulkunja* dakhin batasey dulichhey kanpichhe
	275	Bidaye niye giyechhilem	Ke go tumi, — 'ami *bakul*'
Bichitra	126	Amra khunji khelar sathi —	Amra nachi *bakultalaye*
Bhanusingher Padabalee	5	Sajani sajani radhika lo,	Gantha *bakulmalika*
	8	Gahana kusum-kunja-majhe	*Bakul* joothi jati re
Natyageeti	27	Oi janalar kachhey	Saradin dharey *bakuler* phul
	43	Madhur milan	Hesey akul holo bakul-kanan
	127	Amra door akasher neshaye matal	*Bakulboner* gandhe akul

Part	*Song number*	*Original song*	*Relevant line*
Prem O Prakriti	34	Purano sei diner katha	Bajiye banshi gan geyechhi *bakuler* talay
	67	Orey bakul parul,	Orey *bakul* parul
	70	Abelaye jadi esechha	Ghana *bakuler* mlan beethikaye
	74	Ogo jaler ranee,	Jao go byakul *bakulboner* mukul-anjali
	96	Nirjan ratey nihshabda charanapatey	Pushpa-jhara *bakuler* daley

BOT

(BANYAN TREE)

The Banyan tree is considered one of the oldest and most extensively-growing trees in India,which originates in peninsular India and sub-Himalayan forests. There is hardly any other plant surpassing it as a shade tree. In hot summer days, it gives adequate relief to exhausted pedestrians by providing shelter underneath its wide canopy of dense foliage. The English name has its origin in the word *banias* (the businessmen) who used to take shelter under such trees while moving from place to place in connection with their business. Due to its vastness and long span of life covering even centuries, it is called 'Akshaya bot' or the immortal banyan tree. The reason behind it is that numerous aerial adventitious roots, known as prop roots develop from its spreading branches, which on reaching the ground extend in girth and act as permanent supporting pillars to the branches. The tree may thus, survive even without the main trunk. It is intimately related to the Hindu mythology occupying an impatant place in religion and art of India. In the Bengali month of *Jaistha* (May-June) on the day of *Botsavitri* festival, married Hindu women worship the tree. In ancient times during the Buddhist period, it was also worshipped for getting children. Sometimes great and noble persons are compared with the tree to specify the height of greatness.

There are records of the vastness and life span of the banyan tree in various parts of India. Among these mention may be made of its existence in Kengeri near Bangalore, in the Jamnagar district of Gujarat, in Anantapur district of Andhra Pradesh, in Hosangabad district of Madhya Pradesh and in Arabpur village (Natna) near Karimpur (District: Nadia) in West Bengal. But of all these the 250-year-old (or even more) "The Great Banyan Tree" of the Indian Botanic Garden, Howrah, West Bengal, has become a tree of wonder and admiration because of its age and vastness. It is known to cover an area of 3.5 acres with nearly 2000 proproots, 425 m canopy, 30 m length of the highest trunk and its continued proliferation even without its main trunk (recorded to be of 15 m girth) which was damaged and lost many years ago.

Normally the tree reaches a height of 15-30 m or more — with numerous spreading branches sending down many aerial roots to touch the ground. Leaves large (10-20 cm), broad, ovate with short and stout stalks. Banyan leaves fall in winter and new leaves appear during February-March. Flowers enclosed in a small spherical structure in a special type of inflorescence which on maturity turns into multiple fruits of deep red or scarlet colour. Its bark, young buds, seeds and fruits have medicinal properties. It is propagated by seeds, cuttings and air-layerings.

There is one curious species belonging to the same family of banyan tree known as 'Krishna bot' or 'Krishna's Butter Cup' (*Ficus krishnae*). It bears large, elliptic leaves (15-20 cm) forming a cup on the dorsal surface at base. The legend behind these cup-shaped leaves is that Lord Krishna in his younger days, used to take butter (*nani*) in the sockets of these leaves from the milk-maids.

Part	*Song number*	*Original song*	*Relevant line*
Pooja	82	Amra tarei jani	Tari lagi *boter* chhayay asan pati
	199	Ami marer sagar	Oi paretei jabe taree *chhayaboter* chhaye
Swadesh	1	Amar sonar Bangla,	Kee anchal bichhaechha *boter* mooley, (7)

Part	*Song number*	*Original song*	*Relevant line*
Prakriti	107	Bhor theke aj badal chhutechhe	Jhiki jhiki kari kanpitechhe *bot* (3)
Bichitra	85	Doordeshee sei rakhal chhele	Amar bate *boter* chhayaye (2)
Bhanusingher Padabalee	6	Bondhua hiya por ao re !	Ithi chhilo neeraba banshi *bototata* (8)

BANAPHUL, BANALATA

(WILD FLOWERS AND WILD CLIMBERS)

"Chai na gneyan, chai na janitey
sansar, manush kaharey baley
boner kusum phutitam boney
shukaye jetam boner koley"

Neither have I any desire for enlightenment nor do I feel any urge to know men and human family. I used to bloom wild in forests or remote areas in a jungle, away from human habitats and got dried up in the lap of forests.

Wild flowers in forests, far away from the civilized world, never seek any appreciation of people or society and blossom at their own whim. They may not have the glamour of sophisticated flowers of the civilized society in respect of bright colour or pleasant aroma but their inherent qualities are revealed only when someone looks at them very intimately.

In lyrics, no specific mention has been made of any particular flower as 'Banaphul'. As such specific botanical identities of such plants cannot be ascertained. Tagore's Banaphul may be one or a number of flowers, which he might have noticed growing wild and uncared. He has given names to two such flowers as Peyalee and Banpulak (details given in chapter: 'Plants and flowers named by Tagore').

Another wild flower might have drawn attention of the poet which is locally known as Ghentu or Bhanti (*Clerodendron infortunatum*). It bears white flowers with rosy or violet tinge, faintly scented and blooming during winter and spring. The following citation from Tagore's writing reveals his appreciation for this plant. 'Bhantiphul (a wild flower) is found in plenty in and around Bolpur (Santiniketan). Why don't you plant them ? Those are Vaishnaba flowers of unparalleled beauty and scent. (Letter to Mira Devi, letter # 63, Chithipatra, 4). (Translated version).

Besides those mentioned above, some other flowers found wild along waysides and other open fields in and around Santiniketan unnoticed and uncared, might have drawn attention of the poet as 'Banaphul.' Such plants are probably:

Argyreia campanulata — a shrub bearing pink-mauve flowers in summer and monsoon.

Lantana camara – Bushy shrub bearing variously coloured flowers almost throughout the year.

Ruellia tuberosa – A dwarf shrub or herb bearing mauve-blue flowers almost throughout the year.

These ornamental plants are presently grown in many gardens for their attractive colours.

Similar might have been the case of "Banalata" which does not indicate any specific climber but any among the large number of local, unidentified wild climbers grown in and around Santiniketan. Some such climbers are:

Ipomoea palmata (Railway creeper) – A perennial plant. Its leaves are small (5-7 cm), serrated and flowers are violet, blooming in summer and the monsoon.

Ipomoea learii (Blue dawn flower) – Its leaves are large (8-12 cm), serrated and flowers are bell-shaped, bluish-violet, blooming almost throughout the year, more during summer and the rains.

Ipomoea purpurea (Morning glory) – This flower has been discussed in detail in the chapter: 'Plants and flowers named by Tagore' under "Peyalee."

Ipomoea quamoclit (Cypress vine) – It is an annual climber; its leaves are divided into numerous slender, threadlike segments with tubular flowers, small (2-3 cm), deep red, blooming throughout the year, more in summer and the rains.

Mimosa pudica (Sensitive plant) –This plant is a spreading undershrub with light blue and red flowers, blooming almost throughout the year. The plant is very sensitive.
To botanists, however, *Banalata* or wild climbers specify some of the speces of *Rosa, Clematis* etc. One such plant, *Rosa moschata* (synonym: *R. brunoni*), also known as Himalayan Musk Rose is found in the Himalayas. It bears white and yellowish scented flowers.

Part	*Song number*	*Original song*	*Relevant line*
Pooja	534	Ogo sundara, ekada kee jani	Ami *Banaphul* tomar malaye chhilam tomar gale
Prem	56	Ogo shono ke bajay	*Banaphuler* malar gandha banshir taney mishe jay
	368	Bnodhu tomay korbo raja torutaley	*Banaphuler* binodmala debo galey
	388	Sajabo tomare he	Nanabaraner *Banaphul* diye diye
Prakriti	226	Aj dakhin-batasey	Nam na jana kon *Banaphul*
Bichitra	88	Hyadey go Nanda-ranee	*Banaphule* ganthbo mala
Bhanusingher Padabalee	9	Satimira rajanee	Ganthe *Banaphulmala*
Natyageeti	2	Hridaye rakho go debee	Bishanna kusumakul *Banaphul boney*
	4	Kshama karo morey sakhee	Kshudra ei *Banaphul* prithibee kanoney
Prem O Prakriti	18	Hasi keno nai o nayaney	Shudhaichhe *Banalata* kato katha akul bachaney
Pooja O Prarthana	20	Aji enechhe tanhari asheerbad prabhat kirane	Anande *tarulata** noayichhe matha

* Tarulata: Though in general, it indicates trees and climbers (taru = trees, lata = climbers), but it has a specific botanical identity — *Ipomoea quamoclit.* Tagore however, used it in general term, as may be revealed in the above lyrics.

BANS, BENU

(BAMBOO)

"Ami benu, amar shakhaye
neerab je hay kato na gan."

I am a bamboo flute. Countless songs, alas, lie tongue-tied in my hollow stems.

Since ancient times bamboos have greatly contributed to the development of forests and landscaping in India. When in group, they create a serene and sublime environment which very often inspires the poets and lyricists. These are one among the most widely available group of plants in West Bengal. Bamboo groves beside ponds and streams in rural Bengal, provide partial or relative darkness in and around the place, imparting an oriental effect. Darkness around, rhythmic swing of leaves in gentle breeze, wild oscillation of plants in storm, a low and indistinct sound – all these create a mystic and romantic atmosphere.
These are quick-growing, evergreen, hardy and woody, bushy foliage plants with stout stems (culm) reaching a height of 10-12 m, variable according to species. Nodes give rise to several laterals from which many tall, narrow, light, bright green and drooping leaves are produced. New leaves almost look like grasses. Many such plants when grown in dense groups create a forest look. Flowering may occur after 20-30 years varying with

the species. In the small spikelets (3-3.5 cm) arranged in a branched inflorescence (panicle), 3-6 bright green flowers develop. The plants are known to bear flowers mostly during summer though sometimes it may occur in other seasons also. Life span of a species comes to an end after completion of flowering.

The plants are also of great economic and commercial value. Paper industry is mostly dependent on bamboos. "Ektara" and "dotara" – special musical instruments of the *Bauls* of Bengal- are made of *Dendrocalamus strictus* (English: solid bamboo) and 'flutes' are from *Melocanna bambusoides*. In general, three species—*Bambusa balcooa, Bambusa arundinacea* and *Bambusa bambos*—are extensively grown as bamboos. The plants are propagated by seeds and suckers.

Part	*Song number*	*Original song*	*Relevant line*
Prem	69	Ekla bosey hero tomar chhabi	*Benu* chhaya tomar chelanchale
	190	Sei bhalo sei bhalo	*Benubanachhaya* hoyechhe madhur –
	196	Panthopakhir rikta kulaye	Rater haoaye marmarita *benu-shakhar* daley
	249	Sakaruna benu bajaye ke jay	Sakaruna *benu* bajaye ke jay
Prakriti	16	Modhyadiney jabey gan	He rakhal *benu* tabo bajao
	67	Ei sakal belar badal andharey	Utal haoa *benu* shakhay
	69	Aji barsharater sheshey	*Benuboner* mathay mathay
	96	Chaley chhalo chhalo nadeedhara	Kotha doore *benuban* gay
	108	Neel nabaghaney asharh gaganey	*Oi benubana* doley ghana ghana
	110	Aji pallibalika	*Benumarmara* mukhar pabaney
	197	Orey grihabasee	*Benubanamarmara* dakhina batasey
	199	Ogo badhoo sundaree	Ullas-utarol *benubana* kallol

Part	*Song number*	*Original song*	*Relevant line*
Prakriti	204	Ogo dakhin-haoa	Ami pather dhare byakul *benu**
	218	Dakhin-haoa jago jago	Ami *benu*, amar shakhay neerab je hay kato na gan
	230	Ebar bidaybelar sur dharo	*Benubaner* byakul shakha
	240	An go tora kar kee achhe	*Benur* shakha taley matal patar nachey
	265	Phaguner poornima	*Benubaney* kanpe chhaya
Bichitra	93	Adhek ghumey nayan chumey	*Benur* pata mishay gatha
	130	Amra chash kori anandey	*Bansher* boney pata nadey
Sanjojan	139	(Ami) Shrabana akashey oi	*Benubana* marmare marmarey
Anushthanik	18	Eso eso praner utsabey	Dakhin bayur *benu* rabey
Chitrangada	1	Bela jay bahia	Harin chhutey *benuban* chhaye
	6	Trishnar shanti sundar kanti	Kampita *benubaney* malayer chumban
Bhanusingher Padabalee	10	Bajaore mohan banshi	Radhamoy taba *benu*
Natyageeti	129	Suni oi runujhunu	Jhillijhankrita *benubana* chhaya
Prem O Prakriti	86	Jani jani esechhoe pathey	*Benushakha* andolaney
Pooja	594	Jani go, din jabey	Pather dharey bajbey *benu*
Bichitra	15	Ei to bhalo legechhilo	E je amar *bansher banshi*
Natyageeti	83	Tomar koti-tater dhati	*Benur* panchani

---

*Tagore has occasionally used *benu* to indicate flute.

MADHUK, MOHUA

(MOHUA TREE, INDIAN BUTTER TREE)

"Re mahua, namkhani gramya tor,
loghu dhwani tar
ucchashire tabu rajkula banitar
gourab rakhiba urdhe dhorey.
* * * *
Ami to dekhechhi torey
vanaspatigoshtheemajhey aranya sabhaye
akunthita maryadaye achhis dandaye,
* * * *
kane kane kohi tore
bodhoore jedin pabo,
dakibo 'mahua' nam dhorey."

Oh, mahua ! your name bears a rustic charm and simplicity, a light tone, yet the dignity and elegance of a woman of royal family has been elevated. I have seen you standing in a majestic style among all other forest trees, raising your head high. Let me whisper into your ears — the day I find my 'love', I shall be calling her Mahua.

Madhuk is a tall tree indigenous to India and distributed mostly in dry forest areas of various agro-climatic regions. The tree has a wild beauty, more suitable as a forest plant rather than an ornamental specimen. It attains a height of about 20m and produces clusters of leaves at branch-ends. Leaves are shed in winter and new leaves and flowers appear in spring. Flowers are also borne in clusters near branch-ends during spring and summer. Floral stalks are green or pink; drooping, cup-shaped flowers are scented, rusty or yellowish in colour. Short-lived flowers bloom at night and drop in plenty before sunrise, which are usually picked up by tribals, santhals and other rural folks for future use. Fruits are egg-shaped, initially green in colour turning to yellow or orange when ripe. It is propagated by seeds.

Mahua flowers are edible—raw or cooked. A country liquor is prepared from dry flowers and ripe fruits.

The plant's intoxicating influence on tribal women has been narrated in the following lines of Tagore's poem "Mahua" (*Rabindra Rachanabali* vol. II, 1982, p. 809)

"Tor surapatra hotey banyanaree
sambal sangraha kare poornimar
nrityamattatari.
Re atal, re kathin,
kemone gopane ratridin
taral jaubanbanhi majjay
rakhiachhili bhorey'.

Oh! from your chalice tribal women collect their youthful dancing impulse of a full moon night. The symbol of firm and unflinching determination, how could you keep your overflowing excitement of youthful passions guarded so secretly inside you.

Part	*Song number*	*Original song*	*Relevant line*
Bichitra	93	Adheka ghumey nayana chumey	Kapot dakey *madhuk* shakhey

MADHABEE, MADHABIKA

(MADHABI)

This impressive, woody, spreading ornamental plant, a native of India, is one of the choicest climbers grown in Indian gardens for its dense foliage and fragrant flowers. As it is a very heavy climber, it requires strong support in a sunny location.

Madhabee is evergreen with brown stems. Its leaves are large (15 cm), opposite, arranged in pairs, ovate or elliptic, smooth, dark green with pointed tips. Flowers are fragrant, pinkish-white and yellow on axillary or terminal raceme. Among the five petals, four are almost equal, white in colour and the fifth one is smaller and pale yellow. Flowering is profuse during winter to summer which may prolong up to monsoon. It is propagated by cuttings of young shoots, air-layerings and seeds.

Tagore sees the plant as a pleasant and fragrant gift of spring, as is evident in the following lines of his short poem offered to "Madhabee"

"Madhabee tumi je dakhin bayure
madhuree korechho dan,
se tomarey tai naba naba surey
diye gechhe tar gan."

Oh, madhabee, you have added sweetness to the southern wind. It has offered you in return, songs of diverse nature in novel tunes.

Part	*Song number*	*Original song*	*Relevant line*
Prem	75	Purano janiya cheyo na amare	*Madhabeekunja* bar bar kori bonolakshmeer dala deye bhori
	86	Ami chini go chini tomarey	Tomaye dekhechhi *madhabee* ratey
	105	Noopur beje jaye	*Madhabee* bitaner chhaye chhaye
	130	Ebar milan haoaye haoaye	*Madhabikar* kundi guli ano tuley
	161	Milanrati pohalo,	Phalguner *madhabee-leela* kunja chhila ghire
	169	Keno re etoi jabar twara —	Ekhoni *madhabee* huralo ki sobi
	188	Ke amare jeno	Emon koriya kemaney katibey *madhabeerati*
	220	Ogo kishor, aji tomar dwarey	*Madhabee* tai asila seje
	227	Aji dakshinapabaney	*Madhabeelataye* bhasha hara byakulata
	233	Ogo swapna-swaroopinee,	Sedineri *madhabee-boney* ajo temni phul phutechhe
	279	Likhan tomar dhulaye hoyechhe dhooli	*Madhabee* shakhyaye uthitechhe duli duli
	326	Gharetey bhramar elo	*Madhabee* jaglo boney
	332	Kon debata se	*Madhabeeboner* madhu-gandhe modita
Prakriti	188	Nababasanter daner dali	Latar bandhan haraye *madhabee* morichhe kende
	197	Orey grihabasee	*Madhabeebitaney* bayu gandhe bibhole
	201	Ami path bhola ek pathik esechhi ....,	'Laba ami *madhabee'*
	212	Dinsheshey basanta	Jhara *madhabeer* sathey jaye se je choley

Part	*Song number*	*Original song*	*Relevant line*
Prakriti	225	Tomar bas kotha je pathik	O *madhabee*, O malatee !
	243	He madhabee, dwidha keno,	He *madhabee*, dwidha keno
	245	Phaguner nabeen anande	*Madhabeer* madhumoy mantra
	250	Klanta jakhan amrakolir kal	*Madhabee* jharila bhoomitale
	261	Madhabee hathat kotha hotey elo	*Madhabee* hathat kotha hotey elo
	265	Phaguner poornima	*Madhabeer* manjaree mone ane barey barey
	271	Amar malar phuler	An *madhabee* malatee ashokmanjaree
Prem O Prakriti	90	Amra jhorey-pada phuladal	*Madhabee*ballaree karun kallole

RANGAN

(IXORA)

Some of the species of *Ixora,* viz., *chinensis, coccinea, arborea,* etc. are in general, known as Rangan in Bengali. The name *Ixora* originates from *Ikvara*—a Sanskrit word, indicating the name of a Malabar idol to which flowers of some of the species are offered.

These are popular, ornamental, evergreen, flowering shrubs of small, medium and taller sizes (1.5 – 3.5 m). Rangan leaves are green, simple, and mostly without hair. Flowers in fascinating range of colours – white, pink, scarlet, yellow and rose—are arranged in terminal or axillary clusters almost throughout the year, mostly during summer and monsoon. They retain their freshness for a longer duration for which they are sometimes used as cut flowers.

However, these are mostly cultivated as decorative garden plants, as ornamental hedges and also as potted plants. Propagated by seeds and cuttings.

Part	*Song number*	*Original song*	*Relevant line*
Prem	45	Hey sakha, barata peyechhi	Dekha dao champakey *ranganey*
	69	Ekla bosey hero tomar chhabi	Rang chhadalo prafulla *ranganey*,
Prakriti	271	Amar malar phuler daley achhe lekha,	An karabee *rangan* kanchan rajanee-gandha prafulla mallika

RAJANEEGANDHA

(TUBEROSE)

"Rajaneegandha pushpadanda
uthichhe deerghadehey,
antarmajhe namrata tar
achhe nirmal snehey."

Floral stalks of Rajaneegandha rising up in its tall stature. Its modesty drenched with pure love and affection lies in the depth of its heart.

There are few flowers around us with a poetic name as *Rajaneegandha* (Tuberose). The name is true to its character, as in Bengali, "rajanee" means night and "gandha" indicates sweet smell, i.e., a flower with a delicately fragrant smell at night. The English name tuberose, implies the tubular shape of the flower in the middle. It is a native of Mexico and distributed in almost every corner in India and in many regions of West Bengal. The colour and fragrance of the flower make it a symbol of purity and heavenly qualities.
The herb reaches a height of about 1 m with grass-like, narrow, long, spreading leaves. Its flowers are white, fragrant, emerging in pairs around the central inflorescence, blooming mostly during summer and the rainy season, sometimes throughout the year.

Apart from garden decoration the flowers are used in floral crafts, garlands, bouquet and also in social and religious ceremonies. An essential oil obtained from these flowers, is of high commercial value. The plant is propagated by bulbs.
An association of romanticism with the sweet fragrance of flowers of tuberose, has been expressed in the following lines in Tagore's dance-drama *Shyama* where Utteeya, Shyama's admirer, gives expression to his feelings for her :

"Rajaneegandha agocharey
jemon rajanee swapaney-bhorey sourabhey"

Like the sweet-smelling flowers of Rajaneegandha (tuberose), which unknowingly fill the night with sweet dreams, (Shyama also unconsciously infuses rosy dreams into Utteeya's mind.)

Part	*Song number*	*Original song*	*Relevant line*
Prem	12	Nidrahara rater e gan	Kon *rajaneegandha* hotey anbo se tan kanthe purey
	43	Amar jeebana patra	*Rajaneegandha* agocharey jeman rajanee swapaney bhorey
	52	Aji godhuli laganey	*Rajaneegandhar* parimaley
	94	Chander hasir bandh bhengechhe	O *rajaneegandha* tomar gandha-sudha dhalo
	101	Dinashesher ranga mukul	Eso nibid milankshaney *rajaneegandhar* kananey
	287	Deep nibey gechhe mamo	*Rajaneegandhar* gandha bharechhe mandirey
Prakriti	241	Phagun haoay haoay	Poornima sandhaye tomar rajanee-gandhay
	271	Amar malar phuler daley	*Rajaneegandha* prafullamallika
Natyageeti	98	Ei to bhara holo phuley phuley	Ratri jagar *rajaneegandha*

LABANGALATA

(LUVUNGA)

This climber, though not grown extensively in Indian gardens, has become famous in this region since ancient times because of its inclusion in poet Joydev's "Geetagovinda":

"Lalita labangalata
parisheelana komala malaya-sameere"

The gentle breeze has become sweet in association with the delicate labangalata.

The plant is an annual climber with hook-like, curved thorns on the stem. Its leaves are compound, usually in group of three leaflets. These soft and smooth leaflets of lanceolate, oblong or other shapes, are borne on strong, tubular and long petioles (5-12 cm). Due to large size of the leaves, they swing freely with breeze. Labangalata flowers are small, white, tubular and scented, and the outer part is cup-shaped with 4-5 teeth. The tip is wavy, looking like cloves. Flowering occurs during spring (February to April). Its fruits are yellowish and oblong—known as "Sugandha kokila." The plant is raised from seeds.

Part	*Song number*	*Original song*	*Relevant line*
Prem	322	Elem natun deshey	Matbey dakhin baye manjarita *labanga*-lataye

Ecstatic southern wind will get itself absorbed in great excitement in the maddening company of sprouted labangalata.

Opinions differ on the identity of labangalata. In the plant catalogue of two reputed plant distribution centres in Kolkata (West Bengal) – the Agri-Horticultural Society of India and the Imperial Nursery—*Pergularia odoratissima* has been cited as labangalata. In *Bharateeya Banoushadhi* (Biswas, K.P. and Ghosh, E., 1950, 1973) and also in *The Treatise on Indian Medicinal Plants* (Chatterjee, A and Pakdashi, S., 1994), it was *Luvunga scandens.* In *A Dictionary, Bengali – Sanskrit – English, Caxton Publication, 1987, Limonia scandens* has been referred to as labangalata. I prefer the name *Luvunga scandens* to specify this plant.

 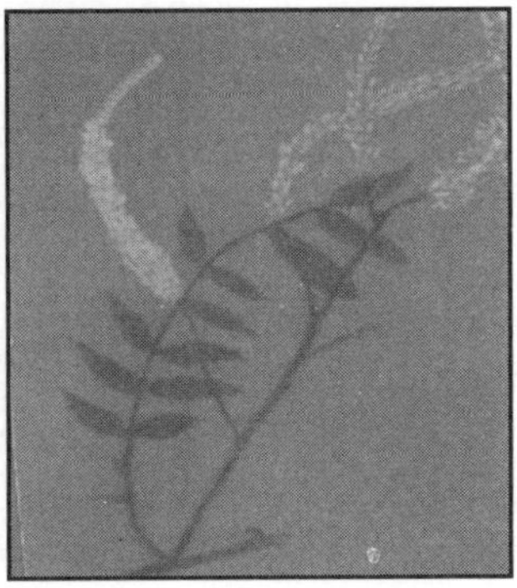

SHAMEE

(SAMI)

Many traditional stories are popular in India on this plant. A native of India and grown mostly in rural areas and in some conservation centres of Bihar, West Bengal and few other states, it is botanically known as *Acacia suma*,.

It is a tree of medium size (5-8 m) with whitish bark and feathery foliage. About 400 tiny, pale green, linear leaflets (5-7 mm) are arranged in pinnae of the compound leaves. Long, drooping, floral spikes with white petals near twig ends are seen almost throughout the year, mostly during the rains and winter. The tree has been much in use as fuel wood in ceremonial occasions and to serve the domestic requirements of rural folk.

Another medium, thorny, evergreen tree (*Prosopis cineraria*) has also been suggested as shamee in Sanskrit and Bengali. It has drooping branches of brownish colour and the wood is very hard. Tiny flowers are seen in winter and the fruits are borne in the rainy season. These plants are mainly used as hedges and firewood.

Between the two species, *Acacia suma* shows the quality of the traditional shamee. Both the plants are propagated by seeds.

Part	*Song number*	*Original song*	*Relevant line*
Prem	65	Ghumer ghana gahan hotey	*Shameeshakhar* bakska hotey jeman jwaley agni

SHARA

(PIN-REED GRASS)

The tree is botanically known as *Saccharum bengalense*. In Sanskrit, *shara* indicates arrow, representing the true nature of the plant. It is found in almost every warm region of India in the states of West Bengal, Bihar, Orissa and others along lakes, ponds and other natural water reservoirs.

It is a large, erect, grassy plant of perennial habit reaching a height of 3-4 m. Its leaves are about 1.5m, narrow at apex, green with rough margin. Tall and white floral clumps are found during the rains. Panicles are 50-90 cm—pale cream to reddish purple. The plant is propagated by seeds and divisions.

Along fallow lands and river banks of Bengal, these plants, when grown in groups, look like a forest and the thin, long and narrow leaves swing with the thrust of air making a low indistinct sound. The plant parts are used in some religious and ceremonial occasions in Bengal. Its leaves are required during sacred thread ceremonies of the Hindu Brahmins. Shara fibres obtained from leaf sheaths are used in rope making.

Part	*Song number*	*Original song*	*Relevant line*
Prakriti	1	Bishwabeena-rabe bishwajan mohichhe	Nadee teere *sharbaney* uthey dhwani sarasara maramara

SHAL

(SAL)

Let *shal* be known to us as follows:

"Ogo maha-shal, tumi subishal kaler atithi, akashere dao sanga barna rangey shakhar bhangitey, bataserey dao moyitree pallaber marmar sangeete, manjareer gandher gandooshey. Jugey jugey kato kal pathik esechhe tabo chhayataley, bosechhe rakhal, shakhaye bendhechhe need pakhi, jay tara path bahi asanna bismriti-paney, udaseen tumi achho chahi."

Oh Shal the great, you are here for several decades giving company to sky with the great colourful branches, offering friendship to air with rhythmic murmuring of leaves and fragrance of flowers. Travellers have enjoyed the shade through the ages, cowboys have taken shelter underneath, birds have formed nests on the branches. They all have passed along the avenue shaded by you, only to be forgotten soon, but you remain indifferent to all such things.

The tree, though not much in cultivation in gardens, grows extensively in the forests of West Bengal and some other states of India. In Sanskrit, it is known as '*Aswakarna*' because of its leaves, which probably resemble a horse's ear .(*Aswa* = horse, *karna* – ear).

It ia a large tree usually 15-25 m in height with reddish brown bark, fissured longitudinally. Its leaves are large (15-20 cm), ovate at base and narrow at apex. Green foliage persists throughout the year excepting the spring season. Shal flowers are terminal and axillary, white or light yellow in colour, faintly scented and generally seen from March onwards. The fruit is reddish or pale yellow. The plant is propagated by seeds.

The timber industry is largely dependent upon shal trees for its basic raw material. The leaves of the plant are used as country plates and dishes.

Part	*Song number*	*Original song*	*Relevant line*
Prem	80	Anmona, anmona,	Jhilli jemon *shaler* boney
	111	Tomar moner ekti katha	*Shaler* beethikaye bari bohey jaye
	181	Marana re, tunhu mamo shyama saman	*Shal*-tal-taru sabhaya-tabadha saba –
Prakriti	31	Shanwana gaganey ghora ghanaghata	*Shal*-piyaley tal-tamaley
	34	Aj bari jhare jhara jhara	*Shaler* boney thekey thekey
	42	Asharh, kotha hotey aj	*Shaler* bonkey mataye
	63	Oi je jharher megher koley	Amey jamey shireesh *shaley*
	125	Ogo saontali chhele,	*Shaler* chhayar dharey
	221	Bhanglo hasir bandh	*Shal* beethikaye chhaya genthey
	250	Klanta jakhan amrakolir kal,	Saurabhdhoney takhan tumi hey *shal* manjaree
	260	Neel akasher koney koney	*Shal*-piyaler boney boney
	267	Orey bakul, parul,	Orey *shal*-piyaler bon
	275	Bidaye niye	*Shaler* boney bharey

Part	*Song number*	*Original song*	*Relevant line*
		giyechhilem	bharey
Bichitra	15	Ei to bhalo legechhilo	*Shaler* boney kshyapa haoa
	41	Amader Shanti-niketan	Moder shaler chhayabeethi
Prem O Prakriti	67	Orey bakul parul	Orey *shal*-piyaler bon

SHIMUL
(SILK COTTON TREE)

"Je basante utkanthita dine
sada elo chanchal dakshiney;
* * * *
shimul pagol hoye matey,
ajashra aiswarya bhar bhare tar daridra shakhatey,
patra kori pura
akashey akashey dhaley raktaphen sura"

The restless southern wind is enlivened on that anxious spring day.... Shimul (red silk cotton tree) goes mad in a frenzy of ecstatic jubilation. Poor or defoliated branches, fully laden with profuse and majestic blooms, seem to have filled its bowl full to the brim pouring frothy, blood-red wine into the sky from the overflowing vessel.

Although shimul has been mentioned only once in Tagore's lyrics, his affinity to the red silk cotton is well known as revealed in his songs and poems.

Three species of silk cotton trees are in cultivation – *Bombax ceiba* (Red silk cotton tree), C*eiba pentandra* (white silk cotton tree) and *Cochlospermum religiosum* (Yellow silk cotton tree). The Red shimul is a native of India. It is a large tree (15-20m) producing showy, bright crimson or red flowers in early spring under complete defoliated condition. It is one of the finest ornamental trees in India in spring-summer.

The White shimul is a large-sized deciduous tree, 15-20 m or more in height, native to tropical regions of America, Asia and Africa. Its trunk is buttressed at base and the branches are green and prickly at young stage. White or red, flowers of this species bloom in winter.

The Yellow shimul is also a native to India. It is a small-or medium-sized (5-10m) deciduous, soft-wooded tree with 5-lobed, palm-shaped leaves. The cup-like Yellow shimul flowers are bright yellow on terminal clusters, emerging in early spring.

All the species are grown in gardens, roadsides and avenues. Besides ornamentation, the floss from seed pods is used for stuffing cushions, pillows and mattresses.

Part	*Song number*	*Original song*	*Relevant line*
Prakriti	275	Bidaye niye giyechhilem	Tumi ke go - "Ami *Shimul*"

SHIREESH

(SIRIS, FRYWOOD TREE, WOMAN'S TONGUE TREE)

" Ekta shireesh phuler gache
agagoda phule bhore achhe, gandhey
bhur bhur korchhe. Shireesh phul
jemon chamatkar dekhte temni
sundar gandha"

There stands a siris tree in full bloom, profusely scented. The siris flowers are not only beautiful but their sweet fragrance is equally pleasing.

This is how Tagore admired *siris*. Mention of *siris* flowers may also be found in our old literatures – *Meghdoota* and *Shakuntala* by Kalidasa, the famous poet of ancient India. In **Meghdoota*, it has been mentioned that women of Aloka used *siris* flowers as earrings and in *Shakuntala*, there are instances of women adorning their hair with *siris* flowers.
It is a large ornamental, deciduous flowering tree (10-20m) with umbrella-shaped crown and attractive foliage. The leaves bipinnate with many pairs of small leaflets (2-4 cm) are pale green and blunt. The leaves fall at the end of winter (January to March), when dry pods are found hanging. New leaves spring up at March

end and blooming starts by the middle of spring and continues till summer. The sweet scent of flowers travels to distant places during night time.

The flowers are greenish-white or pale yellow with numerous, long, white fibre-like stamens turning to pale yellow later on. These protruding stamens give the flower a soft, pleasing, powder-puff-like appearance.

The tree is native to tropical Asia and Africa. It is grown almost in every part of India – in gardens, roadsides and avenues. Various parts of the plant are of economic and medicinal importance. It is propagated by seeds.

Part	*Song number*	*Original song*	*Relevant line*
Prakriti	63	Oi-je jhader megher kole	Amey jamey *shireesh* shaley
	191	Enechho oi shireesh bakul	Enechho oi *shireesh* bakul
	199	Ogo badhoo sundaree	*Shireesher* hindol,
	205	Akash amaye bharlo aloye	Orey *shireesh*, orey *shireesh*, mridu hasir antaraley gandhajaley shoonya ghiris
	226	Aj dakhin batasey	*Shireesh* tomar bhorbey saji
	243	He madhabee, dwidha keno	*Shireesh* shihari uthe
	260	Neel akasher koney koney	Phiris mete *shireesh* boney
Bichitra	81	Pranganey mor shireesh shakhaye	Pranganey mor *shireesh* shakhaye Nacher matan laglo *shireesh* dale

Part	*Song number*	*Original song*	*Relevant line*
Natyageeti	129	Shuni oi runujhunu	Papiya dakey, pulokita *shireesh* shakhey

---

"In (Kalidasa's) *Meghaduta*, women of the city of Alaka are described as holding a lotus in hand, putting on sirisa flowers in ears and the kadamba flowers in parting of hairs...... . In *Ritusamhara* Kalidasa gives charming descriptions of indigenous beautiful trees of India. He said that flowers added beauty to young girls. In the rainy season women decorate their heads with garlands of kadamba, kesara, kakubha and ketak flowers." (Banerjee, S.C. *Flora and Fauna in Sanskrit Literature*, 1980).

SHEPHALI, SHIULI, SHEPHALIKA

(NIGHT JASMINE, SIULI)

Expression of Tagore on Shephali or Shiuli in poems or lyrics as cited below reveal the poet's feelings for this plant.

The Siulis are gloomy, trembling and frightened—taking shelter in the lap of forests, anticipating the arrival of a hard-hearted guest in their forest during winter months.

"Lalit rager sur jharey tai shiulitaley"

It seems that tunes in the raga lalit are falling in drops of minute particles at the base of a siuli tree.

When my bushes of Night jasmines (shephali), in an autumn night, are in a frenzy of jubilation under an aromatic influence.

The sweetly scented shiuli flowers in bloom by the touch of autumn dew, indicate the advent of a favourite festive season in Bengal. The tree is famous for its exceedingly fragrant night-blooming flowers, borne in small dense clusters at stalk ends. The fallen flowers in early morning form a white carpet underneath the tree which are gathered at dawn for various social, religious and domestic purposes. In Sanskrit, it is known

as Parijat because of its heavenly qualities.
It is a dwarf, bushy, ornamental flowering tree of 5-6m in height. Its leaves are rough and green above, whitish and pubescent beneath, with margin distantly toothed. The flowers are small, wheel-shaped, delicately fragrant with united white petals and orange floral tubes; flowering occurs from September to January, blooming at night and dropping off next morning. The plant is propagated by seeds and cuttings.
Shuili flowers are offered in worship and used for making floral crafts. The orange tubes often yield a dye for colouring clothes. The tree is native to India, Siam, Sumatra and Java and grown in public and residential gardens of West Bengal, Assam, Bihar and Orissa.

Part	*Song number*	*Original song*	*Relevant line*
Pooja	346	Deoa neoa phiriye deoa	Amar sharatrater *shephali bon* souravetey matey jakhan
Prem	13	Amar kantha hotey	Sharat kanpe *shiuli-phuler* harashey
	23	Chhutir banshi bajlo	Bandhan tutey uthbey phutey *shiuliguli*
	53	Ami chahitey esechhi	Anek kunda anek *shephali* bhorechhe tomar dala
	124	Keno jaminee na jete	Hero go *shephali* porhichhe jhoriya,
	139	Aha, jagi pohalo bivaboree	Ganthi laho anchaley naba *shephalika*
	162	He kshaniker atithi,	Jhara *shephalir* patha bahiya
	166	Sakalbelar aloye bajey	Shishirshihar sharat pratey *shiuliphuler* gandha sathey
	170	Jani jani holo jabar ayojon	*Shiuliboner* madhur stabey
	288	Tumi amaye dekhechhiley	Likhon tomar binisutor *shiuliphuler* mala,

Part	*Song number*	*Original song*	*Relevant line*
Prakriti	141	Aji sharata tapaney	Oi *shephalir* shakhey kee boliya dakey
	144	Amra bendhechhi kasher guchchha	Amra genthechhi *shephalimala*
	146	Amar nayana-bhulano eley,	*Shiulitalar* pashey pashey
	147	Shiuliphul, shiuliphul	*Shiuliphul, shiuliphul*
	150	Ogo shephaliboner	Ogo *shephaliboner* moner kamana
	151	Sharata-alor kamalboney	*Shiuliboner* udas bayu
	153	Sharat, tomar arun alor anjali	*Shiuliboner* buk je othey andoli
	157	Hridaye chhiley jegey,	Se je oi *shiulidaley* chhadalo kanantaley,
	159	Dekho dekho, shuktara ankhi meli chaye	Dak diyechhey re *shiuliphulere* –
	160	Olo shephali,	Olo *shephali*
	162	Ebar abagunthan kholo	*Shiulisuravi* ratey
	163	Tomar nam jani ne,	Sara bela *shiulibone*
	164	(Mori lo) kar banshi	Hridaykunjaboney munjarila madhur *shephalika*
	165	Amar rat pohalo	Shesh korey dao *shiuliphuler* marana-sathey
	167	Alor amal kamalkhani	Lalit rager sur jhorey tai *shiulitaley*
	177	Shiuli phota phurolo jei	*Shiuli-phota* phurolo jei
	185	Sheeter boney kon se kothin	*Shiuliguli* bhoye malin boner koley

Part	*Song number*	*Original song*	*Relevant line*
Bichitra	19	Amarey dak dilo ke	Ashwiney oi *shiulishakhey*
	91	Tumi ushar sonar bindu	Sharat-prater pratham shishir pratham *shiuliphuley*
Prem O Prakriti	6	Golap phul phutiye achhe,	*Shephali* hotha phutiye
	76	Charanarekha tabo	Chhilo to *shephalika* tomari lipi-likha

SHYAOLA, SHAIBAL

(ALGAE)

"Ganguli mor shaibaleri dal —
ora bonyadharay path je haray
uddam chanchal"

My songs are like a mass of floating algae. They lose their direction by the thrust of floodwater, indomitable and vibrant.

Nobody is inclined to welcome algae, everyone is eager to get rid of them. They are branded as one of the undesirable and unacceptable plants in the society. These plants belong to a group of non-flowering, and chlorophyll-bearing aquatic species, which are able to produce their own food (autophytic) and cannot be differentiated into roots, stems and leaves (thallophytes). These algae primarily represent the species of the following genus: (1) *Chlamydomonas* (Family: chlamydomonadaceae), (2) *Volvox* (Family: Volvocaceae and (3) *Spirogyra* (Family: Zygnemataceae. Most species are fresh water forms and grow abundantly in standing water of ponds, pools, ditches, lakes, tanks, etc. Sometimes, because of their growth in great abundance, the whole water surface of the pond looks green. Some species are free floating and roll freely in water as tiny green balls. Though majority of Algae are free floating, a few remain attached to the substratum. They grow on moist tree trunks, moist soils, old walls and stone near stagnant water which itself is considered as its safest abode. The plants may be unicellular or multicellular; they are multiplied by sexual and asexual means.

In the lyric, "*Ganguli mor shaibaleri dal*" (Prem 5), Tagore feels that his own songs are like floating algae. As these plants never care to nourish themselves by anchoring at a fixed place, finding pleasure only as floaters and aimless movers towards infinity, Tagore believes that his songs have the same characteristic qualities as exhibited by these floaters and movers.

Part	*Song number*	*Original song*	*Relevant line*
Prem	5	Ganguli mor	Ganguli mor *shaibaleri* dal
	8	Orey amar hriday amar	Jadas ne *shaibaler* jaley
Bichitra	13	Jakhan padbe na mor	*Shyaola* esey ghirbey dighir dhargulaye

SOJNE

(DRUMSTICK)

"Ganyer akash sojne phuler hatchhanitey dakey amaye.
Phuray ni, bhai, kachher sudha,
nai je re tai doorer kshudha ...."

The sky over rural area, beckons me with floral clusters of sojne (drumstick). There is no dearth of nectar around me, thus no longing for a distant place.

The plant does not have any ornamental use. It is a popular vegetable in some states of India including West Bengal and also a native of India. In Sanskrit, it is known as Shovanjan.
It is a small-to medium-sized tree, 4-6m in height. In its branches, large leaves are scattered with many leaflets, which are shed in winter followed by the appearance of new leaves. The clustered flowers from the axils of new leaves are small, creamy white or yellowish white and scented, visible during late winter and spring. These drooping clusters of flowers are highly impressive and appealing. The fruit (40-50cm) resembles the shape of a drumstick and hang in clusters ripening from April to June, hence the popular name. Sojne plants are raised from seeds and cuttings.

Although drumstick flowers may not be comparable with colourful ornamental flowers, their inherent qualities and gentle appeal make them so popular and acceptable in their own abodes – villages. Tagore finds it impossible to ignore their attractiveness in their own habitats. The lines cited above express the poet's admiration for drumstick flowers most appropriately.

Part	*Song number*	*Original song*	*Relevant line*
Bichitra	15	Ei to bhalo legechhilo	Ganyer akash *sojne* phuler hatchhanitey dakey amaye

SORSHEY

(SARSON)

"Neel digantey" oi phuler agun laglo,
basantey souraver shikha jaglo
* * *
sorshey kshetey phul hoye tai jaglo
* * *
sorshey kshetey dheu hoye tai jaglo"

The blue horizon displays a blaze of colourful floral fire, the flame of sweet spring has risen up.... In the sarson field it shows an assemblage of flowers.... In the sarson field it comes up as waves.

It is an annual, herbaceous, edible, oilseed crop of low height. This small oilseed crop is botanically known as *Brassica campestris* var, *sarson* and popularly as yellow sarson. It originates from North-East India or China and mostly grows in West Bengal, Bihar and Orissa. In winter, exceedingly beautiful, deep yellow or pale yellow flowers on a vast patch of deep green, lively plants in the fields under the blue sky, swing like waves by such mass assemblage of flowers, in an appropriate natural background, making the sarson field ablaze with its flower colour. This has been uniquely expressed in his song "*Neel digante oi phuler agun laglo"* ("Prakriti," 262). No other flower would perhaps suit here other than sarson to unfold the essence of the theme in its proper perspective.

Part	*Song number*	*Original song*	*Relevant line*
Prakriti	262	Neel digante oi	*Sorshey* kshetey phul hoye tai jaglo *Sorshey* kshetey dheu hoye tai jaglo

SNEUTI
(HIMALAYAN MUSK ROSE)

"Haimanteer meyer nam rekhechhi
sneuti, kintu parichay jani ne"

I have given a name to Haimanti's daughter after Sneuti but its identity is yet unknown to me.

In another letter (*no. 42, Pathey O Pather prantey*), it has been revealed that the poet could not trace the correct identity of the plant even after several queries (vide Introduction). He was probably attracted by the name itself and used it in lyrics and verses.

In Sanskrit, the plant is known as Sevantee. It is a large, thorny, climbing rose, botanically known as *Rosa brunonii* and distributed in Central and West Himalayan regions up to an elevation of 3000m. It bears small (5 cm), white, scented flowers with musky odour and grows in profusion from late winter to summer. It produces ovoid, rosy red or deep brown fruits.

The flowers are a source of attar and rose water. The hard and porous wood of the seunti tree is used for making walking sticks. The plant is propagated from cutting, layering, budding and grafting.

Part	*Song number*	*Original song*	*Relevant line*
Prem	165	Okey bandhibi ke re	Shishire bhara *sneuti* -jhara geetey
Natyageeti	130	Ei to bhara holo phuley phuley	Champa chameli *sneuti* beli

HENA

(HENNA, EGYPTIAN PRIVET, TREE MIGNONETTE)

"Bhor holo jei shravana sharbaree
tomar bedaye uthlo phutey henar manjaree"

As the day dawned after a Shravana night (second month of the rainy season in Bengal), clusters of henna flowers began to bloom along the fence of your enclosure.

It is a multi-branched, tall shrub (up to 4 m) with dense foliage. It originates from north Africa and south-west Asia. In gardens, it is mainly used for tall hedges.
The plant has woody, angular stems, greyish-green when young. The leaves are small (2-6 cm), opposite, lanceolate, without any hair. The apex is narrow and the petiole stout. The flowers are profuse small (0.5 cm), fragrant, light yellow, greenish or white. They are borne in terminal clusters during summer and rains, occasionally in other seasons too.
The leaves are the source of a dye known as henna or mehendi, which are often used by women for colouring palms and for dyeing hair. Henna oil is used in perfumery industry. For dense hedges, it should be pruned after flowering. The plant is propagated by seeds or cuttings.

In some quarters night jasmine (*Cestrum nocturnum*), a bushy shrub, native of West India, bearing white, greenish yellow, fragrant flowers, is known as Hena.
Tagore in his lyric has, however, used the *Tree mignonette* to specify Hena.

Part	*Song number*	*Original song*	*Relevant line*
Prakriti	75	Bhor holo jei shrabana sharbaree	Tomar bedaye uthlo phutey *henar* manjaree
	266	Ek phaguner gan se amar	Shudhaye tarey bakul- *hena*

PLANTS AND FLOWERS NAMED BY TAGORE

Tagore's world was never limited by geographical boundaries. In his songs, dramas or poems, he collected material from exotic sources whenever necessary and made them look like a natural part of his own language, culture and tradition. His love for nature, plants and flowers was so intense that he did not only appreciate the qualities of flowers already known to him, but whenever he found a flower – ornamental or wild, indigenous or exotic he immediately expressed his eagerness to know its local name. If not properly satisfied, he coined a meaningful and sonorous name. Even a well known flower was sometimes given a name to his liking. Some such plants and flowers are listed below:

Agnishikha (Glorylily)

It is botanically known as *Gloriosa superba* and is indigenous to India, Malay and Indonesia. It is a bulbous climbing plant blooming in summer and the rains and continuing up to autumn. The flower is greenish yellow, turning to orange and scarlet. The colour of flower resembles a flame, hence the name, *Agnishikha* (flame of fire). It is also known as 'langul' to the tribals. (Chattopadhyay, D.P. , *Santiniketan* : *Uttarayan*, 1988, p. 29-30).

Tarajhara (Fallen stars)

"Samnei lata bhorechhe sada phuley
— biliti nam,mone thake na —
nam diyechhi tarajhara; — rater
belay gandha tar phulbaganer pralaper
moto. Ebar se phutechhe akale,
sabur soyni sheet phurobar"

(Tagore, Rabindranath. 'Sambhasan" Shyamali, Rabindra Rachanabali *vol. III, 1983, p. 395)*

The climber nearby is thoroughly covered with a mass of white flowers. At times it becomes difficult to remember foreign names.

I've named it Tarajhara; at night it emits a sweet smell much like getting absorbed in a frenzy of excitement in a flower garden. This season it has bloomed untimely, not waiting for the winter to be over.

According to D.P. Chattopadhyay, botanist, Santiniketan, Tarajhara represents *Vinca rosea (Catharanthus roseus* 'Alba'). In English it is known as Madagascar periwinkle. It is a dwarf, ornamental shrub bearing starlike white flowers throughout the year.

But it does not fit in with Tagore's own description of the plant "Sambhashan," *Shyamalee,* where he mentions that it is an exotic climber bearing white scented flowers. This time it has bloomed untimely, not waiting for the winter to be over. As he cannot remember its English name, he has named it tarajhara* (fallen stars) for its starlike sparkling white flowers. Thus the plant as referred to is a climber, not shrub, blooming normally after winter.This may be *Clematis gouriana* (clematis), an ornamental climber native of India and Malay. It bears profuse tiny, white, scented flowers (2-3 cm) in clusters or in trees.

---

* Tarajhara literally means fallen stars, perhaps for the resemblance of its sparkling white flowers with stars.

Neelmonilata (Purple wreath)

A native of tropical America it is a heavy ornamental climber, botanically known as *Petrea volubilis.* Deep blue flowers in clusters bloom at the end of winter and continues up to summer. "Knowing that Tagore had great fascination for blue flowers, his close associate and friend Dr. W.W. Pearson brought this creeper from Latin America, the poet named it '*Nilmonilata.*" (Ghosh, P.K. *et al, Tagore and Flowers,* 1993, p. 78). Tagore offered his deep regard to this flower in his poem 'Neelmonilata' in *Bana-banee.* He says:

"Neelrange amar gabheer ananda, tai ei phuler banee amar jatayater pathey pratidin amakey dak diye stabdha korechhe. Amar dik theke kabiro kichhu balbar ichhe hoto kintu nam na

pele sambhashan kara chaley na. Tai latatir nam diyechhi neelmonilata."

(Tagore, Rabindranath. "*Neelmonilata" Banabanee, Rabindra Rachanabali* vol. II, 1982, p. 857).

I've a special fondness for blue colour. Hence the message of these flowers used to draw my attention during the course of my daily stroll, forcing me to stop in response to its call. As a poet I always cherished a desire to express something but in absence of a name it is difficult to address. That is why I named the climber Neelmonilata.

In Pathe O Pather Prante, Tagore had expressed his desire to take lessons on life from '*Neelmonilata*' as it never had shown any signs of fatigue in preaching its message.

"*Amar dwarer kachhe neelmonilata je uchchhwasita banee akashe prachar korchhe aj paryanta se ektuo klanta hotey janlo na. Ami oikhan theke amar jeebaner mantra nitey chai, kono gurubhar gurubakya thekey noy – gachh jemon korey pata meley diye akasher alo thekey adrishya achinhita pathey dekey ney apnar pran apnar tej.*"

(Tagore, Rabindranath, *Pathey O Pather Prante (1938), Rabindra Rachanabali* vol XII, 1989, p. 501).

The Neelmonilata near my doorstep, has been preaching an impassioned message to the sky since long, it is not tired till yet. I like to take my lesson on life from it only and not from any unbearably weighty advice of someone – much in the same way the plant gathers its elixir of life and vigour from light of the sky in an invisible and uncharted way.

The name Neelmonilata (spectacular blue vine) was given for its fascinating blue or purple flowers.

Peyalee (Morning glory)

"Amakey ene dilo oyi buno charagachhti.
Patar rang holde-sabuj,
phulguli jeno alo pan karbar
shilpakara peyala, beguni ranger.

Prashna kori, nam kee,
jabab nei konokhaney.
* * *

Ami okey dhorey enechhi ekti dak namey
amar ekla janar nibhrite.
Or nam Peyalee."

Brought me that wild sapling. Leaves yellowish green, flowers violet, in the shape of a cup of artistic skill, pretending to drink light. "What's your name," I asked. No answer from anywhere....

I adopt it, giving a pet name to satisfy myself in my solitude in quest of knowledge. Its name is Peyalee.

It is botanically known as *Ipomoea purpurea*, an annual climber, a native of tropical America. It grows very quickly, comes into flowering within 3-4 months after seed sowing. The flowers are violet, blue or red (8-12cm), cuplike, blooming in the morning and fading in the evening. This particular variety flowers in autumn and winter. Tagore named it peyalee (a cup)because of artistic and cup-shaped or funnel-shaped look of its flowers. (*Patraput*, 8).

Banpulak (White Paveta)

Banpulak is a tall shrub distributed in the foothills of the Himalayas, South India and some parts of West Bengal. Botanically, it is known as *Pavetta indica,* in Sanskrit – *Papat* and in Bengali *kukurchurha.* The leaves are narrow at both ends with hairy surfaces. The flowers are white and scented, borne in clusters in terminal cymose inflorescence from late winter to monsoon. Banpulak roots have medicinal value. The name Banpulak (joy of forest) was probably given for the wild look of the plant which brings joy in forests with its clustered white and scented flowers.

The poet in his letter to Hemantabala Devi mentioned:

"Ei samaytatei (basanta) ar ek jater sada phul gol gol manjareetey shakhar granthitey granthitey utphulla hoye othey.

Ekhankar loker kachhe tar parichay jijnasa korley boley bunophul, nam jana nei. Amra sei anadrita jangal thekey aniye baganey lagiyechhilam ekhon tar puraskar pachhi. Soundarya sougandhe – bahudoor paryanta kritagnata bistar korechhe. Ami er nam diyechhi banapulak".

(Tagore Rabindranath, *Chithipatra 9, "Patra" (letter) 135, March 8, 1934)*

During this season (spring), another type of white flower in ball-shaped branches, arising from the nodal regions of branches show signs of great happiness and pride. Local residents when asked about its identity reply that these are wild flowers—the exact name is not known to them. We brought the plants from their disrespectful and forlorn jungle and planted them in the garden. Now we get the reward. With their beauty and sweet smell they express gratitude reaching to far-flung corners of the region. I have named it Banpulak.

Basantee (Bird's eye bush)

This evergreen shrub, *Ochna jabotapita*, is a native of tropical Asia. In Bengali it is known as Ramdhanchanpa. It attains a height of about 3 m bearing yellow flowers (5 cm), several together, with persistent sepals, greenish initially and turning to red gradually.The fruit is black in colour and very attractive. Golden yellow flowers appear during spring and continue up to summer.

"It is a small ornamental tree common in Santiniketan and named Basanti by Tagore". (Ghosh, P.K. *et al*, *Tagore and Flowers*, 1993, p.59). The name Basantee (spring delight) signifies the coppery red leaves and scented orange or godlen yellow flowers, waking up in spring by the soft vernal air.

Madhumanjaree (Rangoon creeper, Honey Wreath)

"Ei latar kono ekta bideshee nam nishchay achhe – janine, janar darkar nei. Amader desher mandirey ei latar phuler byabohar chaley na; kintu mandirer bahirey je debata muktaswaroopey

achhen tanr prachur prasannata er madhye bikashita. Kavya swaraswati kono mandirer bandinee debata non; tanr byaboharey ei phulkey lagabo thik korechhi; tai natun korey nam ditey holo. Roope rase er madhye bideshee kichhui nei; ei desher haoaye matitey er ektuo bitrishna dekha jai na, tai dishi namey ekey apan korey nilam."

(Tagore, Rabindranath, "Madhumanjaree" *Bana-banee, Rabindra Rachanabali* vol. II, 1982, p. 863)

This climber must have a foreign name – I do not know, nor do I feel any urge to know. In temples of our land, flowers of this climber are not used in worship. But there is enough evidence that it is accepted with great complacency by the Almighty outside the temple, which is free from every bondage. Kavya Saraswati (goddess of learning) can never be a deity in captivity inside any temple; I have decided to offer these flowers to her; as such new name has to be given. There is nothing foreign, in its beauty and appeal; it is not averse to the soil and climate of this region. Therefore, I make it my own by giving it a local name.

It is a heavy, woody, ornamental climber native of Malaysia. It is botanically known as *Quisqualis indica*. It bears flowers on long, pendulous clusters – axillary or terminal, initially white, turning to pink and finally red, blooming profusely during spring, summer and monsoon.

It is commonly believed that Tagore's 'Madhumanjaree' and the prevalent Bengali names—Haragouree or Madhumalatee—are one and the same. (Kar, Sadhana, *Rabindrasahitye Phul, Amrita,* October 1965.) Prof. Debidas Bhattacharjee and Shri D.P. Chattopadhyay also hold the same view (Samanta, Rabindranath, *Rabindra Kavye Phul*, 1977).

In the poem "Madhumanjaree", Tagore says that he has struck up a friendship with the climber by naming it *Madhumanjareelata.*

'Nam diye ami nilam apan korey — Madhumanjareelata'

(*"Madhumanjaree", Banabanee, Rabindra Rachanabali* vol II, 1982, p. 864)

It has been named Madhumanjaree (Honey wreath) probably because of its beautiful pendulous floral clusters.

Shwetmoni souravee (Sweet pea)

This ornamental climber is botanically known as *Lathyrus odoratus*. It is an annual climber bearing odorous, white, blue, violet, maroon and red flowers in winter. Naming of the plant as above, by Tagore, has been indicated in *Rabindrakavye Phul* (Samanta, Rabindranath, 1977, p.3). Swetmoni souravee literally means choicest, white, scented flowers referring to the white flowers among others exhibited by the plant.

Sonajhuri (Australian wattle, Golden shower)

It is an ornamental tree, a native of tropical Australia. Its botanical name is *Acacia auriculiformis*. In Bengali it has another name too – Akashmoni. The tree is quick growing, 10-15m in height. Its modified midribs are actually the leaves in absence of true leaves (phyllodes). The flowers are yellow and scented borne near the end of branches. Profuse flowering is seen in autumn (September – October) but occasional flowering continues almost throughout the year. In a booklet published by Visva-Bharati, it has been indicated that the name *Sonajhuri* has been coined by Tagore. (Basu, S.K. and Dutta, R.M., *Trees of Santiniketan*, 1957, 21). Sonajhuri (Golden shower) signifies the graceful golden yellow flowers in dense spikes near the end of branches.

Himjhuri (Indian cork tree)

"Ekhon asadh jamiyechhe himjhuri phul. O namta amarie deyoa nam, lamba brintawala sada sada phul, kebolie jhorey jhorey podchhe gach talaye. Deergha unchu gach, nimer moto pata, phuley sada hoye gechhe tar shikhar ... gandhati sumishta."

(Samanta, Rabindranath, *Rabindrakavye Phul*, 1977)

The flowers of Himjhuri now appear to be in a festive mood. I have named it, ... long-stalked white flowers dropping incessantly at the foot of the tree. A tree of great height with leaves much alike those of a neem tree, the top looking completely white ... pleasant smell.

Botanically known as *Millingtonia hortensis,* this tree is a native of Myanmar. In Bengali it is also known as Akashnim. It is an evergreen ornamental plant bearing beautiful greenish white, fragrant flowers in terminal clusters in autumn and spring. From *Trees of Santiniketan* (Visva-Bharati publication) and *Rabindrakavye phul* (Tagore Research Institute publication), it is known that the name *Himjhuri* to this tree was given by Tagore. The tree has been named Himjhuri because of its snow-white, fragrant, drooping mass of flowers, in long, terminal panicles.

Baganbilas (Bougainvillea)

It is a group of woody, ornamental, climbing shrub, conspicuous for brightly coloured bracts. Different varieties of this group originate from three natural species and two hybrid species – all known to be native plants of South America. On suitable supports the plants can climb up to 15-20 metres. Baganbilas leaves are green, simple, alternate, generally ovate with stiff thorns at the axils. The flowers are small, inconspicuous, tubular, arising generally in groups of 3-9 on showy coloured bracts. Its flowering period and quality of bloom vary with species, variety and location.

It has been mentioned in the book *Tagore and Flowers* (Ghosh, P.K. *et al*, 1993, p.70) that the name 'Baganbilas' was given by Tagore.

The name means "luxury of the garden." Its showy and colourful bracts are indeed a source of pleasure in gardens.

Phuljhuri (White poinsettia)

That the name Phuljhuri for the plant *Euphorbia leucocephala* was given by Tagore is also known from the book *Tagore and Flowers*. It is a medium-to-tall shrub (2-3m), a native of Mexico and West Indies. Its slender, pinkish branches produce soft, narrow, small-sized, oblong to elliptic light green leaves, usually in whorls.

Phuljhuri flowers are small and yellowish with beautiful, obovate, white bracts. When the plant is in bloom from late autumn to early spring, the entire plant seems to have a snow-white cover. The name *Phuljhuri* suggests its resemblance to a dazzling *tubri* or *phuljhuri* (a firework emitting starlike sparks) when in full bloom with its brilliant snow-white flowers.

Jati (Philippine violet)

It is a dwarf (1-1.5 m), bushy, spreading shrub with ovate-lanceolate or elliptic leaves, which are green above, pale beneath with hair on both upper and the lower surfaces. Its flowers are violet, purple or white depending on the variety, appearing in clusters at the end of axillary lateral branches, the corolla tube funnel-shaped (5 cm) with five lobes. Most Jati flowers begin to bloom from early winter and may continue till spring or summer. 'Tagore honoured it with this Bengali name' *(Tagore and Flowers, p. 54)*.

Kanta nageshwar (Acacia sp)

The identity of this plant is difficult to assume for lack of detailed information. As per Pratima Devi's recollection in "Rabindranath's

Love for Flowers" *(Prabasi*, 1966), it is known that Tagore was very fond of thorny plants like cacti and he earmarked a plot exclusively for them. A thorny plant like Babul Acacia (*Acacia nilotica*) brought from Tripura, was planted there. It is assumed that the plant under reference could have been the Sweet Acacia or West Indian black thorn (*Acacia farnesiana*), a native of West Indies. It is a thorny shrub or small tree popular in gardens. This ornamental plant is commonly used for putting up hedges around gardens. It bears bright golden yellow, sweet-scented, round, showy, small flowers (1-1.5 cm) in the axil of leaves, 1-3 in number, from November to March. Pods nearly cylindrical. This plant has been listed in "*Trees of Santiniketan" (Visva-Bharati*, 1957, p. 20).

It appears that this plant might be the " Kanta Nageshwar" though Nageshwar as applied here does not, in any way, resemble 'Nagkeshar' (*Mesua ferrea*), except for the facts that flowers of both the plants are scented with a touch of golden yellow colour.

Indumallee

Tagore makes a mention of this plant in his poem Abedan.

"...hetha tabo dakshiner batayantaley
manjarita indumallee ballaree –
bitaney,..."

(" Abedan" Chitra, Rabindra Rachanabali, vol. I, 1980, p. 609)

Here, at the base of your southern window, clusters of indumallee are in bloom.

Perhaps nothing is indicated in the above lines to suggest the identity of this plant, excepting that it is a climber bearing flowers in inflorescence. In *Rabindrakavye Phul* (Samanta, Rabindranath, 1977), it has been mentioned that as per a Bengali dictionary (*Shabdasagar abhidhan*), *Indumallee* is somlata (Moon plant) and chandraballee is madhabee (*Hiptage benghalensis*). Probably Tagore has used partial combination of these two plants while naming Indumallee, though its identity still remains unclear.

Besides plants as above, a number of exotic flowers find place in his literary works without undergoing any change, viz. Carnation, Pansy, Dahlia, Gerbera, Fuchsia, Geranium, Rhododendron, etc. Again, some exotic flowers have been used with partial modification, in his poems viz. "'Nargesh" (Nargis) and "Ispani." There is a reference of the former in the poem "Phulobala" (*Shaishab Sangeet, Rabindra Rachanabali* vol. II, 1983, p.1012). The plant is a bulbous herb known as *Narcissus* which originates from Europe, North Africa and Western Asia. In India it may be seen in bloom in Kashmir, Himachal Pradesh and in valleys of higher altitudes in Uttar Pradesh. The flowers are white, in various shades of yellow or a combination of yellow and orange, scented, blooming in winter and spring. The most popular species in India is probably, *Narcissus tagetta.*

The only source of identity of *Ispani,* is part of a letter written to Dinendranath Tagore from Buinos Aires. The following poem is a part of the letter:

'Door prabasey sandhyabelay basay phirey enu,
hatath jeno bajlo kothay phuler buker benu.
Anti panti khunje sheshey bujhi byaparkhana,
baganey sei juin phutechhe chirodiner jana.
Gandhati tar puropuri Bangladesher banee,
ektuo to dey na abhas ei deshi ispani.
Prakashye tar thak na jatai sada mukher dhang,
komalatay lukiye rakhey shyamal buker rang."

("*Chithi"Purabee, Rabindra Rachanabali,* vol. II, 1982, p. 682).

At this far-off place abroad, when I came back to my dwelling in the evening, suddenly I felt a familiar scent of a flower somewhere. After vigorous searching I could find out the source; the pleasant small emanates from jasmines in full bloom inside the garden. The sweet scent preaches the essence of Bengal fully, though the ispani of this region does not match with it even indistinctly in spite of its bearing sweet, delicate and refreshingly white flowers.

The above information, only reveals that the flower is exotic, white, fragrant and soft. This smell reminds the sweetness of jasmine. In *Rabindrakavye Phul* (p. 94), the plant has been referred to as a species of *Xanthoxylum*, a native of Souh America and known as spino in Spain, bearing white, fragrant flowers in November – December. In the same book there has also been a mention of the possibility of *Oncoba spinosa* (Bride of the Desert) to specify the plant. It is a woody shrub or small tree with axillary spines, a native of tropical Africa and tropical America, bearing large, white, fragrant flowers in summer months and usually grown as hedges. However, these are nothing but assumptions.

PLANTS AND FLOWERS IN TAGORE'S SONGS

1. Ashath *(Pipal)*
Page 1

2. Ashok *(Asoka tree)*
Page 3

3. Am *(Mango)*
Page 7

4. Amlokee, *(Amla)*
Page 10

5. Amrha *(Hog-plum)*
Page 12

6. Kachu *(Arum)*
Page 13

7. Kadamba (Kadam *Kadam)*
Page 14

8. Kanakchanpa *(Maple twist)*
Page 18

9. Karabee *(Oleander, Rose bay)* Page 20

10. Kanchan *(Mountain ebony)*
Page 22

11. Kaminee *(Chinese box, Orange jessamine)*
Page 25

12. Kash *(Thatch grass)*
Page 27

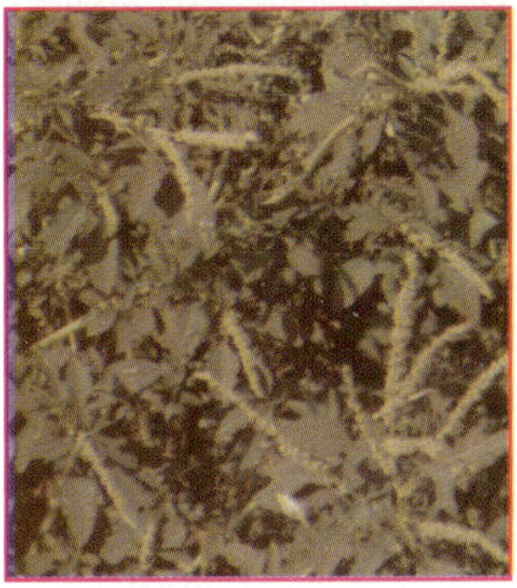

13. Kantalata
(Thorny weeds)
Page 29

14. Kusum
(i) Lac tree
Page 31

14. Kusum *ii) Safflower*
Page 31

15. Krishnakali: Shwet
(Four O' Clock plant)
Page 35

16. Krishnachurha
(Peacock flower)
Page 37

17. Keya *(Screwpine)*
Page 39

18. Golakchanpa *(Pagoda tree)* Page 42

19. Golap *(Rose)* Page 44

20. Chandan *(Sandalwood tree)* Page 47

21. Chanpa Phul *(Golden champa)* Page 49

22. Jaba *(China rose)* Page 53

23. Jam phul *(Indian black berry flowers)* Page 55

24. Juin Jateeya phul *(Jasmines)* Page 57

25. Kunda *(Kund-jasmine)* Page 59

26. Chameli, Jati *(Spanish jasmine)* Page 61

27. Joothee *(Jnui-jasmine)* Page 64

28. Banmallika *(Wild jasmine)* Page 68

29. Bela *(Arabian jasmine)* Page 70

30. Mallika
(Malli-jasmine)
Page 72

32. Jhau
(Casuarina, She-oak)
Page 78

31. Malatee
(i) Malti (non-jui)
Page 74

33. Jhumkolata
(Passion flower)
Page 80

31. Malatee *(ii) Malti (Jasmine)* Page 74

34. Tamal *(Egg tree)*
Page 82

35. Tal, Talee *(Palmyra palm)* Page 85

36. Doorba *(Doob grass)* Page 88

37. Dolonchanpa *(Ginger lily)* Page 92

38. Dhan, Aush *(Rice)* Page 93

39. Dhutro *(Thorn apple)* Page 96

40. Nagkeshar *(Iron-wood tree)* Page 98

41. Narikel *(Coconut tree)* Page 100

42. Neelshatadal *(Blue lotus)* Page 102

43. Padma, Kamal *(Lotus)* Page 104

44. Palash *(Parrot tree)* Page 110

45. Parijat *(Holy tree)* Page 113

46. Parul *(Trumpet flower)* Page 116

47. Piyal *(Cuddapah almond)* Page 118

48. Bakul *(Indian medlar, Spanish cherry)* Page 121

49. Bot *(Banyan tree)* Page 127

50. Banalata *(Wild climbers)* Page 130

50. Banaphul *(Wild flowers)* Page 130

51. Bans, Benu *(Bamboo)* Page 133

52. Madhuk *(Mohua tree)*
Page 136

53. Madhabee *(Madhabi)*
Page 138

54. Rangan *(Ixora)*
Page 141

55. Rajaneegandha
(Tuberose) Page 143

56. Labangalata
(Luvunga) Page 145

57. Shamee *(Sami)*
Page 147

57. Shamee *(Sami)* Page 147

58. Shara *(Pin-reed grass)* Page 148

59. Shal *(Sal)* Page 149

60. Shimul *(Silk cotton tree)* Page 152

61. Shireesh *(Siris, Frywood tree)* Page 154

62. Shephali *(Night jasmine)* Page 157

63. Shyaola, Shaibals *(Algae)* Page 161

64. Sojne *(Drumstick)* Page 163

65. Sorshe *(Sarson)* Page 165

66. Sneuti *(Himalayan musk rose)* Page 167

67. Hena *(Henna, Tree mignonette)* Page 169

PLANTS AND FLOWERS NAMED BY TAGORE

1. Agnishikha
(Glorylily)
Page 171

3. Neelmonilata
(Purple wreath)
Page 172

2. Tarajhara
(Fallen stars)
Page 171

4. Peyalee
(Morning glory)
Page 173

5. Banpulak (White Paveta) Page 174

6. Basantee (Bird's eye bush) Page 175

7. Madhumanjaree (Honey Wreath) Page 175

8. Shwetmoni souravee (Sweet pea) Page 177

9. Sonajhuri (Golden shower) Page 177

10. Himjhuri (Indian cork tree) Page 178

11. Baganbilas (Bougainvillea) Page 178

12. Phuljhuri (White poinsettia) Page 179

13. Jati (Philippine violet) Page 179

14. Kanta nageshwar (Acacia sp) Page 179

15. Nargesh *(Narcissus)* Page 181

16. Ispani *(Oncoba)* Page 181

GLOSSARY OF BOTANICAL AND HORTICULTURAL TERMS

PRIMARY CLASSIFICATION OF PLANTS

In general, the entire plant kingdom may be divided into two major divisions :

1. Phanerogams (bearing flowers and seeds) Two sub-divisions

a) Gymnosperms (naked seeded), viz. pine

b) Angiosperms (bearing flowers and fruits, seeds covered)

Angiospermic plants in two sections:

i) Monocotyledons, (embryo with single cotyledon or seed leaf), e.g. palmyra palm, coconut palm, paddy, etc.

ii) Dicotyledons (embryo with two cotyledons or seed leaves), e.g. mango, pea, gram, etc.

2. Cryptogams (not bearing flowers and seeds)

Three sub-divisions

a) Pterydophyta (ferns)

b) Bryophyta (moss)

c) Thallophyta

i) Algae
ii) Fungi

Nomenclature

For scientific identity, a plant's name bears two parts – genus and species. The botanical name of a banyan tree is *Ficus bengalensis* — *Ficus*, the generic name and *bengalensis*, the specific name. Again, a species may have some varieties based on colour, scent or other such characters.

Parts of a plant

Root: Underground parts for anchoring the plant in soil and drawing nutrients from soil.

Stem: Parts above soil shouldering burdens of the entire structure.

Trunk: Stout, branchless, woody parts of stem just above the soil.

Branches and branchlets: These are the network structure borne by the trunk enabling the plant to receive adequate light and air and arranging translocation of nutrients from stem to leaves and reversely, channelising prepared food from leaves to every sector of the plant body.

Leaf: Borne on branches, prepares food and carries out respiration and transpiration (releasing excess water).

Flower: Reproductive part of a plant body. A modified shoot consisting of modified stems and leaves. The male reproductive organ or stamens consist of filaments and anthers. The anthers contain pollen grains, inside which there are male gametes. On the other hand, the female reproductive organ or carpels consist of stigma, style and ovary. The ovary contains ovule, inside which the ovum is present. The union of the male gamete and ovum gives rise to embryo. The fertilised ovule and ovary ultimately form seeds and fruits, respectively.

Kinds of root

Primary root: Roots developing from radicle as a result of seed germination. This with proper development forms the tap root.

Adventitious root: In case the roots do not develop from the radicle but from other parts of the plant body like stem, leaves, etc., they are termed as adventitious roots.

Prop root: Modified aerial adventitious roots developing from the aerial branches of a banyan tree, coming down straight and fixes up in the soil, increases in girth and ultimately serving as a pillar and sharing the burdens of branches.

Stilt root: Modified adventitious roots developing from the stem of a screw pine in a slanting manner, fixes up in the soil and allows the plant to rest on it.

Fibrous root: In monocot plants, the primary roots either degenerate or their growth is checked. In such cases, several adventitious roots develop from the base of the stem and anchor the plant with soil. Such roots are known as fibrous roots, as in rice.

Nature of stem

Herb: A plant with non-woody, soft and green stems. This may be : –

i) annuals – which exist for one season, e.g. rice, sarson, several flowering annuals.

ii) bi-ennials – which may survive for two seasons, e.g. radish, carrot.

iii) perennials – which survives for more than two seasons, e.g., canna.

Shrub: A plant smaller in height (usually up to 3-4 metre or so), woody but without any distinct trunk, e.g. china rose, ixora.

Tree: A plant above 4 m in height, woody and having distinct trunk, e.g. mango, banyan tree.

Deciduous and evergreen plants

Plants where seasonal shedding of leaves takes place, are known as deciduous plants, e.g. silk-cotton tree, pagoda tree, palas. Plants remaining green throughout the year, periodically shedding their leaves but not at a time, are known as evergreen plants, e.g. Indian medlar, asoka tree.

Kinds of stem

Underground stem: Thick modified stem under the soil surface resembling roots, and getting swollen by storing food. This may be rhizome, e.g. *Hedychium*; tuber, e.g. *Mirabilis jalapa*; bulb e.g. tuberose, corm, e.g. gladiolus. All such bulbous plants having underground modified stems perform functions like storage of food, asexual propagation and overcoming adverse conditions.

Caudex: Stems without branches bearing crown of leaves at the apex, e.g. palmyra palm, coconut.

Culm: Stems with nodes but hollow within, e.g. bamboo, grass.

Sucker: Fast-growing shoots developing underground, suddenly come up forming new plants e.g. chrysanthemum.

Runner: Modified sub-aerial stem, where slender branches arising from the mother plant, run parallel along the surface of the ground up to certain distance and develop new plants there by striking roots and leaves, e.g. doob grass.

Axil: The angle between leaf and shoot.

Axillary bud: Buds developing at the axil.

Apical bud: Buds at the apex of shoot.

Buttress: A projecting support by outer roots at the base of a plant helping to keep it straight.

Creepers and climbers: When a weak-stemmed plant creeps along the ground, it is known as a creeper, e.g. doob grass, and when it climbs up with the help of a support, it is called climber e.g. clitoria, quamoclit. Under stress and strain, a creeper may behave like a climber or vice-versa. Hence, the saying creepers and climbers (like cacti and succulents) broadly covers all types of creeping, crawling, climbing, trailing, rambling and scanding species of plants.

Node: The place of insertion of a leaf on the axis or the region on the stem or branches which bears leaves.

Leaf

Bracts: A small leaf from the axil of which a flower comes out.

Bracts may be:

1) Leafy, like leaves, e.g. Acalypha
2) Petaloid, like petals, and of bright colour, e.g. bougainvillea
3) Spathe or when looking like a green, boat-shaped body covering the inflorescence fully or partially, e.g arum, palm.

Petiole: The stalk of a leaf connecting the leaf blade with the branch.

General outline or shape of a leaf blade or lamina

Linear: Narrow and long, e.g. rice, doob grass.

Ovate: Egg-shaped, e.g. China rose, banyan tree.

Cordate: Resembling heart or betel-shaped, e.g. pipal tree.

Sagittate: Arrow-shaped with the basal lobes directed backwards, e.g. Alocasia.

Lanceolate: Shaped like lance-head, e.g. oleander, bamboo.

Acicular: Shaped like needle, e.g. pine.

Rotund: Wheel-shaped, e.g. lotus.

Oblong: Longer than broad with sides more or less parallel, e.g.banana.

Simple and compound leaves

Simple: Single lamina on a petiole, e.g. mango, China rose.

Compound: When several leaflets are borne by the petiole, e.g. rose, drumstick.

Pinnate compound: When leaflets are arranged on both sides of a rachis like a bird's feather, e.g. siris.

Palmate compound: When the leaflets are arranged on the tip of the petiole or rachis like fingers of a palm, e.g. silk cotton tree.

Bi-pinnate: Leaflets in a compound leaf borne on secondary axes arising from the rachis or midrib, e.g. *Acacia nilotica*, *Mimosa pudica.*

Tripinnate: Pinnate with the pinnae themselves pinnate, and their pinnae again pinnate, e.g. drumstick.

Trifoliate: Three leaflets articulated to the petiole terminally, e.g. oxalis.

Digitate: Consisting of several finger-like leaflets, e.g. silk cotton tree.

Phyllotaxy

Arrangement of leaves on stems or branches.

1. **Alternate**: Arrangement of leaves in which they are placed singly with change of side at each node, i.e. coming one after the other by turns, e.g. mango.

2. **Opposite**: When in a node two leaves come out in opposite direction, e.g. guava.
3. **Whorled**: When more than two leaves develop from the same node, e.g. oleander.

Parts of a flower

A complete flower has usually four whorls:

1. **Calyx**:: The lowermost green whorl, each segment of which is known as sepal.
2. **Corolla**: The second and the most important whorl, each segment of which is known as petal.
3. **Androecium**: The third or the male whorl consisting of stamens, the male reproductive structure having two parts –the filament or a narrow slender structure and anther where pollen grains are formed which are essential for sexual reproduction.
4. **Gynoecium**: The fourth or the female whorl consisting of carpels, the female reproductive structures having three parts –the round tip at the apex is known as stigma, the tubular structure below is the style and the swollen basal portion, the ovary which contains ovules inside, essential for sexual reproduction.

Complete flower: Where all the four whorls are present, e.g. china rose.

Incomplete flower: If any one of the four whorls is absent in a flower, it is said to be incomplete, e.g. tube rose, gourd.

Bisexual flower: When in a flower, both stamens and carpels are present, e.g. China rose.

Unisexual flower: If one among the two reproductive whorls is absent in a flower, it is unisexual, e.g. gourd.

Monoecious plant: Male and female flowers borne separately but on the same plant, e.g. coconut palm, cucumber.

Dioecious plant: Where the two sexes occur on different individuals, the male flower on distinct plant from the female, e.g. palmyra palm, papaya.

Perianth: Calyx and corolla together, especially when not clearly distinguishable, forming a floral leaf.

Thalamus: Region of the floral stalk where the four whorls of a flower get attached, the lower slender part of which is known as peduncle.

Asexual or vegetative reproduction

When new plants are produced from any vegetative part of a plant body. The methods in practice are:

1. **Cutting:** When a portion of any part of a plant body, especially stems, branches or leaves, are cut for generating a new plant under favourable condition by root initiation in the cut-out part.
2. **Ground layering:** By bending branch of a plant to the ground and covering a portion of it (10-15 cm) below the tip with soil giving a notch at a covered portion of the stem.
3. **Grafting:** The process and operation of inserting a part of one plant into another or placing it upon another in such a way that a union is formed and the combination continues growth. When the inserted part is a bud, the operation is known as **budding.**
4. **Air-layering (Gootie):** A practice to cause root initiation on an overground part of a stem while still attached to the parent plant. A ring like cut-out portion of bark of a branch is covered with wet soil or moss followed by a white polythene cover to develop adventitious roots on the cut portion for developing a new plant.

Forms of flower

1. **Campanulate:** Bell-shaped, e.g. gourd.
2. **Funnel-shaped:** When the corolla tube is narrow and the upper part looks like a funnel, e.g. morning glory, *Datura.*
3. **Tubular:** When the corolla tube is narrow and tube-shaped, e.g. tuberose.
4. **Rotate:** Wheel-shaped, e.g. *Calotropis, Nyctanthes.*
5. **Cruciform:** Cross-shaped look of the four petals on the stalk, e.g. sarson.

BIBLIOGRAPHY

English books and articles

Banerjee, S.C. (1980). *Flora and Fauna in Sanskrit Literature*, Naya Prakash, Calcutta.

Basu, S.K. and Dutta, R.M. (1957). *Trees of Santiniketan*, Visva-Bharati.

Bose, T.K. and Chowdhury, B. (1991). *Tropical Garden Plants in Colour.*

*Chakraverty, R.K. and Mukhopadhyay, D.P. (1987). *The Great Banyan Tree,* Bull. Botan. Surv. India, 29 (1-4), 59-70.

*Chakraverty, R.K. and Mukhopadhyay, D.P. (1995). *Gardens in India – a Retrospect, Recent advances in Taxonomy.* Suravi Publications, Jaipur.

*Chakraverty, R.K., Pandey, D.S. and Mukhopadhyay, D.P. (2003). *Directory of Plants in Botanic Gardens of India.* Flora of India (4), Botanical Survey of India, Kolkata.

*Chakraverty, R.K. and Mukhopadhyay, D.P. (In press). *Beautiful Creepers and Climbers*, Botanical Survey of India.

Devadhar, C.R. (1966), *Dramas of Kalidasa*, Varanasi, Motilal Banarasi Dass.

Ghosh, P.K., Bhattacharjee, G.N. and Mondal, S. (1993), *Tagore and Flowers.* Publication and Information Directorate, New Delhi.

Haughton, G.C. (1987), A *Dictionary : Bengali-Sanskrit-English.* Caxton Publication.

Mazumdar, L. and Roy, S. (1988*), Santiniketan – Uttarayan, the Poet's Houses and Gardens.*

Mazumder, L. and Roy, S. (1988), *Jogindranath Chattopadhyay's Reminiscences of Santiniketan Forty Years Ago*, Santiniketan.

Menninger, E.A. (1962), *Flowering Trees of the World* (for tropics and warm climates), Hearthside Press Inc., New York.

Mitra, D.K. (2006), *Gems from Tagore* (A lyrical English translation of selected Tagore songs), East West Publications, New Delhi.

Mitra, R.L. (1990). *Nymphaeaceae*, Fascicles of Flora of India, Fas. 20, Botanical Survey of India.

Pal, B.P. and Krishnamurthy, S. (1967), *Flowering Shrubs*, Indian Council of Agricultural Research, New Delhi.

Pal, B.P. (1972), *Beautiful Climbers of India*. Indian Council of Agricultural Research, New Delhi.

Price List of Plants, Agri-Horticultural Society of India, Calcutta.

Price List of Plants.,Imperial Nursery, Calcutta.

Racova, A. (2001), *My Experience With Translating Tagore and Writers From Bengali*, Anustup, Anya Rabindranath (Spl. edn.), 154-158.

Randhawa, M.S. (1961), *Beautiful Trees and Gardens*, Indian Council of Agricultural Research, New Delhi.

Randhawa, M.S. (1983), *Flowering Trees.*,National Book Trust, New Delhi.

Singh, U., Wadhwani, A.M. and Johri, B.M. (1990), *Dictionary of Economic Plants in India*, Indian Council of Agricultural Research, New Delhi.

Sinha, R.P.N. (1993),*Our Trees*, Publication Division, Ministry of Information and Broadcasting, Government of India.

Swarup, V. (1991),*Garden Flowers*,National Book Trust, New Delhi.

Tree Planting Ceremony in Santiniketan (1984), Rabindra Bhavan, Visva-Bharati.

Useful Plants of India (1986), Publication and Information Directorate, Council of Scientific and Industrial Research, New Delhi.

With India – Raw Materials. *The Wealth of India: A Dictionary of Indian Raw Materials and Industrial Products*, Council of

Scientific and Industrial Research, New Delhi, Raw Materials, Vol. I-XI, 1948-1976.

Bengali books and articles

Bandyopadhyay, Pranab (1964). "*Rabindranather Prakriti O Premer Gane Phul,*" *Desh* (August).

Bhattacharrya, Shibakali (1980-1990). *Chiranjeeb Bonoushadhi* (I-X).

Bishi, Pramathanath (1967). *Desh* (Sahitya Sankhya).

Biswas, Kalipada and Ghosh, Ekkori (1973-1977), *Bharateeya Bonoushadhi* (I-VI).

*Bose, Tarun Kumar, Mukhopadhyay, Debi Prasad, Pal, Dulal Chandra and Chowdhury Bimal (to be published). *Sachitra Udyan Briksha: Ushnamandaleeo O Upa-ushnamandaleeo* (Illustrated).

Chanda, Rani (1981). *Gurudev*, Visva-Bharati.

Chattopadhyay, Debiprasanna (1989), *Santiniketan, Uttarayan.*

Chattopadhyay, Harinarayan, *Rashtriya Shabdakosh.*

Chattopadhyay, Jogendra Kumar, *"Visva-Bharatir Ankur,"* *Prabasee* (February 1939).

Chowdhuranee, Indira Debi (1960), *Rabindra Smriti.*

Das, Tarak Mohan (1962), *Amar Gharer Ashepashe.*

Debi, Pratima, *"Rabindranather Pushpapreeti," Prabasee* (February1956)).

Ghosh, Dhirendranath (1959), *Raktakarabeer Tatwa O Tatparya,*. Modern Book Agency, Kolkata.

Jana, Bimala Kinkar (b. 1399). *Baigyanik paddhatite liliphuler chash.*

Kundu, Debabrata and Pal, Ambuj (1996), *Jana Ajana Udbhider Bijnansammata Nam O Gotra.*

Mukhopadhyay, Ashoke (1988), *Sansad Samartha Shabdakosh, Sahitya Sansad*, Kolkata.

*Mukhopadhyay, Debi Prasad (1999), *Rabindrasangeetey Udbhid O Phul*, Baulmon Prakashan, Kolkata (Illustrated).

*Mukhopadhyay, Debi Prasad (2000), *Kabikrita namey Koekti Deshi O Bideshi Phul,* Anay Rabindranath, Anustup (Special edn.), Illustrated.

*Mukhopadhyay, Debi Prasad (2002), *Rabindrasangeet mey Prayukt Udbhid Aur Phul* (Hindi version). Baulmon Prakashan, Kolkata (Illustrated).

Mukhopadhyay, Hare Krishna (1950) *Kabi Joydeb O Sri Sri Geeta-gobindam.*

Mukhopadhyay, Prabhat Kumar (1964), *Rabindrajeebanee* (IV).

Pyne, Santosh Kumar (1994), *Phul Photar Sandhaney.*

Roy Choudhury, Bibhas (1959), *Rabindranather Raktakarabee*, Modern Book Agency, Kolkata.

Samanta, Rabindranath (1977), *Rabindrakabye Phul.*

Sarkar, Nalini Kanta (1941) "Rabindranather Sangeet Srishti," *Shanibarer chithi* (October, Rabindrasankhya), 893-896.

Singh, Ranjit (1995), *Bharateeya Phal*, National Book Trust.

Thakur (Tagore), Rabindranath, *Geetabitan (Akhanda)* 1999, Visva-Bharati.

Thakur (Tagore), Rabindranath, *Rabindra Rachanabali* (I-XV). Paschim Banga Sarkar. (Govt of West Bengal)

Thakur, Soumyendranath (1960), *Kalidaser Kabye Phul.*

* Indicates books or articles where the author is associated individually or jointly.

FLOWERING CALENDAR OF PLANTS AND FLOWERS IN THE TEXT

(As per alphabetical order of names followed)

*Name**	*Scientific name*	*Family*	*Flowering season*	*Flower colour*	*Remarks*
Agnishikha (Glory lily)	*Gloriosa superba*	Liliaceae	Summer, monsoon	Greenish yellow changing to orange, then scarlet	Herbaceous bulbous climber
Ashath (Pipal)	*Ficus religiosa*	Moraceae	Summer	Black/ violet receptacle	Shade tree
Ashok (Asoka tree)	*Saraca asoca*	Caesalpi-niaceae	Spring, summer	Orange-red or yellow then scarlet	Shade tree, flowers faintly scented
Am (Mango)	*Mangifera indica*	Anacar-diaceae	Spring	Greenish yellow	Fruit tree
Amlakee (Amla)	*Emblica officinalis*	Euphor-biaceae	Summer (sometimes up to September)	Greenish yellow	Fruit tree

*English names in parenthesis.

Name	*Scientific name*	*Family*	*Flowering season*	*Flower colour*	*Remarks*
Amda (Hog plum)	*Spondias pinnata*	Anacar-diaceae	Spring	Yellowish or greenish white	Fruit tree
Kachu (Arum)	*Colocasia esculenta*	Araceae	No speci-fic season	Yellowish white	Bulbous plant
Kadamba (Kadam)	*Anthoce-phalus chinensis*	Rubiaceae	Monsoon	Pale yellow	Ornamental tree, scented flowers
Kanak-champa (Maple twist)	*Pterosper-mum aceri-folium*	Stercu-liaceae	Spring, summer	Yellowish white	Ornamental tree, scented flowers
Karabee (Oleander)	*Nerium oleander*	Apocyna-ceae	Almost all seasons, more in spring to autumn	White, red, rosy.	Ornamental shrub, flowers faintly scented
Kanchan (Mountain ebony)	*Bauhinia* sp.	Caesal-piniaceae	Almost all seasons (depending on species)	White, red, yellowish or violet (depending on species)	Ornamental tree or shrub, flowers scented

Name	*Scientific name*	*Family*	*Flowering season*	*Flower colour*	*Remarks*
1. Rakta-kanchan (Mountain ebony-red)	*B. variegata*	Caesalpiniaceae	February-April	Red dominant	Tree
2. Dev kanchan	*B. purpurea*	Caesalpiniaceae	September-December	Mainly violet	Tree, flowers scented
3. Shwet kanchan	*B. acuminata*	Caesalpiniaceae	March-September	White	Tall shrub
Kaminee (Chinese box, Orange jessamine)	*Murraya paniculata*	Rutaceae	Almost all seasons, more in spring, summer and monsoon	White	Ornamental tall shrub or small tree, flowers scented
Kash (Thatch grass)	*Saccharum spontaneum*	Poaceae	Autumn	White	Perennial grass
Kantalata (Thorny weeds)					

Name	*Scientific name*	*Family*	*Flowering season*	*Flower colour*	*Remarks*
1. Kantikari (yellow berried night shade)	*Solanum surattense*	Solana-ceae	Summer	Blue	Thorny herb
2. Shiakanta (Thorny mimosa)	*Mimosa rubicaulis*	Mimo-saceae	Summer to winter	Blue turning white	A thorny weed
3. Kantanotey (Prickly amaranth)	*Amaranthus spinosus*	Amaran-thaceae			A thorny weed
Kusum (Kusum)	1. *Schlei-chera oleosa*	Sapinda-ceae	Late spring, summer	Greenish or yellow	Tall tree, host for lac insects.
	2. *Cartha-mus tinctorius*	Asteraceae (Compositae)	Winter, spring	Yellow or orange red	Herbaceous edible oil seed crop

Name	*Scientific name*	*Family*	*Flowering season*	*Flower colour*	*Remarks*
Krishna-kali (Four-O'-clock plant)	*Mirabilis jalapa*	Nyctagina-ceae	Summer, monsoon	Many	Herb, scented flowers
Krishna-churha (Peacock flower)	*Caesalpi-nia pul-cherrima*	Caesalpini-aceae	Mostly in spring, summer and monsoon	Reddish yellow or orange red	Ornamental shrub, flowers faintly scented
Keya (Screw-pine)	*Pandanus tectorius*	Pandana-ceae	Late spring to mid monsoon	White	Shrub or tree, flowers scented
Golak-chanpa (Pagoda tree)	*Plumeria*	Apocyna-sp. ceae	Almost all seasons, more in spring to autumn	Red, rosy, white or yellowish	Ornamental tree
Golap (Rose)	*Rosa* sp.	Rosaceae	All seasons, more in winter and spring (de-pending on species)	Many colours (depending on species)	Shrubs or climbers, flowers mostly scented

Name	*Scientific name*	*Family*	*Flowering season*	*Flower colour*	*Remarks*
Chandan (Sandal-wood tree)	*Santalum album*	Santalaceae	Almost all seasons	White then reddish	Rare, endangered species
Champa (Golden champa)	*Michelia champaca*	Magnolia-ceae	Almost all seasons, more in spring to rains.	Yellowish or golden yellow	Ornamen-tal tree, flowers very fragrant
Jaba (China rose)	*Hibiscus rosa-sinensis*	Malvaceae	All seasons	Many	Ornamen-tal shrub
Janti	*Barleria cristata*	Acanthaceae	Winter	Violet, blue or white	Bushy dwarf shrub
Jam (Indian black berry)	*Syzygium cumini*	Myrtaceae	Spring	Greenish white	Fruit tree

Name	*Scientific name*	*Family*	*Flowering season*	*Flower colour*	*Remarks*
Juni (Jasmines)	*Jasminum* sp.	Oleaceae	Almost throughout the year (depending on species)	Mostly white	Ornamental shrub or climber, flowers mostly scented
1. Kunda (Kund-jasmine)	*J. multiflorum*	Oleaceae	Almost all the year round, mostly in early winter to spring	White	Climbing shrub, flowers small/large, scented
2. Chameli/ Jati (Spanish jasmine)	*J. grandiflorum*	Oleaceae	Almost all the year round, more during summer and monsoon	Dusty white	Climbing shrub, star-shaped flowers, scented
3. Banamallika (Wild jasmine)	*J. angustifolium*	Oleaceae	Late winter to summer	White	Climbing shrub, star-shaped flowers, scented

Name	*Scientific name*	*Family*	*Flowering season*	*Flower colour*	*Remarks*
4. Bela (Arabian jasmine)	*J. sambac*	Oleaceae	Late spring, summer and monsoon	White	Shrub, scented flower
5. Mallika (Malli-jasmine)	*J. Sambac* var. mallika	Oleaceae	Spring	White	Shrub, flowers larger than Bela, scented
6. Malatee (Malti)	*J. flexile* (*J.azoricum*)	Oleaceae	Almost throughout the year, more in winter	White	Climbing shrub with scented flowers
7. Joothee (Juin-jasmine)	*J.auricu-latum*	Oleaceae	Spring, summer and monsoon	White	Climbing shrub, star-shaped flowers scented
Jhau (Casua-rina)	*Casuarina equiseti-folia*	Casuari-naceae			Tall pine like tree

Name	*Scientific name*	*Family*	*Flowering season*	*Flower colour*	*Remarks*
Jhumko-lata (Passion flower)	*Passiflora* sp.	Passiflo-raceae	Different seasons depending on species	Variously coloured depending on species	Ornamental tendril climber
Tamal (Egg tree)	*Garcinia xantho-chymus*	Clusia-ceae	Spring	White with feeble yellow shade	Fruit tree, mostly seen in forests
Tarajhara (Fallen stars)	*Clematis gouriana*	Ranun-culaceae	Late winter to monsoon	White	Ornamental dwarf climber
Tal (Palmyra palm)	*Borassus flabellifer*	Arecaceae	Spring	White	Monocot fruit tree
Doorba (Doob grass)	*Cynodon dactylon*	Poaceae	Almost throughout the year	White with violet or red touch	Grass. Very suitable for garden lawn
Dolon-champa (Ginger lily)	*Hedychium coronarium*	Zingibera-ceae	Monsoon	White	Ornamental bulbous plant

Name	*Scientific name*	*Family*	*Flowering season*	*Flower colour*	*Remarks*
Dhan (Rice)	*Oryza sativa*	Poaceae	Autumn and late autumn (Hemanta)	Inflores-cence initially green, on maturity yellowish or reddish	Grassy plant. Major food crop
Dhutro (Thorn apple)	*Datura* sp.	Solana-ceae	Almost throughout the year, more in summer and monsoon	Greenish white	Shrub
Nagkeshar (Iron wood tree)	*Mesua ferrea*	Clusiaceae	Late winter to summer	White	Ornamental tree, flowers scented
Narikel (Coconut tree)	*Cocos nucifera*	Arecaceae	Spring and summer	Pale yellow	Monocot fruit tree

Name	*Scientific name*	*Family*	*Flowering season*	*Flower colour*	*Remarks*
Neelmonilata (Purple wreath)	*Petrea volubilis*	Verbenaceae	Late winter to summer	Blue	Ornamental climber
Neelshatadal (Blue lotus)	*Nymphaea nouchali*	Nymphaeaceae	Almost throughout the year except winter	Blue in different shades	Ornamental aquatic bulbous plant
Padma	*Nelumbo nucifera*	Nelumbonaceae	Mostly in summer and monsoon, sometimes in early autumn	White or red	Ornamental aquatic bulbous plant
Palash (Parrot tree)	*Butea monosperma*	Fabaceae	Spring	Red, vermilion or brown	Ornamental tree
Parijat (Holy flower)	*Erythrina variegata var. orientalis*	Fabaceae	Spring	Deep red	Ornamental tree

Name	*Scientific name*	*Family*	*Flowering season*	*Flower colour*	*Remarks*
Parul (Trumpet flower)	*Stereospermum colais (Syn. S. suaveolens, S.personatum)*	Bignoniaceae	Spring, summer	Deep violet, coppery brown, yellow or yellowish red	Ornamental tree
Piyal (Cuddapah almond)	*Buchanania lanzan*	Anacardiaceae	Late winter to spring	White with greenish shade	Edible fruit tree, mostly grown in forests
Bakul (Indian medlar)	*Mimusops elengi*	Sapotaceae	Spring to monsoon	White or greenish	Ornamental tree
Bot (Banyan tree)	*Ficus bengalensis*	Moraceae	Spring to autumn	Fruits red	Shade tree
Banaphul (Wild flowers)					

Name	*Scientific name*	*Family*	*Flowering season*	*Flower colour*	*Remarks*
1. Peyalee (Morning glory)	*Ipomoea purpurea*	Convolvu-laceae	Autumn and winter	Violet or bluish	Annual ornamental climber
2. Banpulak (White paveta)	*Pavetta indica*	Rubiaceae	Late winter to monsoon	White	Tall shrub
3. Ghentu	*Cleroden-dron infor-tunatum*	Verbena-ceae	Winter, spring	White with rosy or violet tinges	Shrub
4. ”	*Argyreia campanu-lata*	Convolvu-laceae	More in summer and monsoon	Light rose	Ornamental shrub
5. ”	*Lantana camara*	Verbena-ceae	Throughout the year	Various colours	Bushy shrub
6. ”	*Ruellia tuberosa*	Acantha-ceae	Throughout the year	Light blue	Dwarf shrub or herb

Name	*Scientific name*	*Family*	*Flowering season*	*Flower colour*	*Remarks*
Banalata (Wild climbers)					
1. -					
(Railway creeper)	*Ipomoea palmata*	Convolvu-laceae	Summer, monsoon	Violet	Perennial climber
2. – (Blue-dawn flower)	*Ipomoea learii*	Convolvu-laceae	All seasons, more in summer and monsoon	Bluish violet	Perennial climber
3. Tarulata (Cypress vine)	*Ipomoea quamoclit*	Convolvu-laceae	All seasons, more in summer and monsoon	Deep red	Annual climber
4. Lajjabati (Sensitive plant)	*Mimosa pudica*	Mimosa-ceae	Almost all seasons	Light blue or red	Dwarf shrub, very sensitive
Basantee (Bird's eye bush)	*Ochna jabotapita*	Ochnaceae	Spring, summer	Golden yellow	Tall orna-mental shrub

Name	*Scientific name*	*Family*	*Flowering season*	*Flower colour*	*Remarks*
Bans (Bamboo)	*Bambusa* sp.	Bambusaceae	Usually summer	White	Woody tree, economic, foliage grass like
Madhuk (Mohua tree)	*Madhuca indica*	Sapotaceae	Spring	Light yellow or brown	Tall tree
Madhu-manjaree/ madhu-malatee (Rangoon creeper)	*Quisqualis indica*	Combretaceae	Spring, summer, monsoon	White, red, orange	Ornamental climber, flowers scented
Madhabee (Madhabi)	*Hiptage benghalensis*	Malpighiaceae	Late winter to summer	White or yellowish	Ornamental climber
Malatee (Malati)	1. *Aganosma caryophyllata*	Apocynaceae	Summer, monsoon	White	Ornamental climber, star like scented flowers

Name	*Scientific name*	*Family*	*Flowering season*	*Flower colour*	*Remarks*
	2. *Jasminum flexile*	Oleaceae	All seasons, more in winter	White	Ornamental shrubby climber, flowers scented
Rangan (Ixora)	*Ixora* sp.	Rubiaceae	Almost throughout the year, more in summer and monsoon	White, red, yellow, rose, orange, (depending on species)	Ornamental shrub
Rajanee-gandha (Tuberose)	*Polianthes tuberosa*	Agavaceae (Amarylli-daceae)	All through the year, more in summer and monsoon	White	Ornamental bulbous plant with scented flowers
Labanga-lata (Luvunga)	1. *Luvunga scandens*	Rutaceae	Spring	White or pale yellow	Large thorny climber

Name	*Scientific name*	*Family*	*Flowering season*	*Flower colour*	*Remarks*
	2. *Pergularia odoratissima*	Asclepiadaceae	Summer	Greenish yellow	Evergreen climber native to China. Flowers like cloves, scented
Shamee (Sami)	1. *Acacia suma*	Mimosaceae	Throughout the year	White	Medium-sized fuel tree
	2. *Prosopis cineraria*	Mimosaceae	Winter	Pale yellow or cream	Medium-sized fuel tree
Shara (Pin-reed grass)	*Saccharum bengalense* (*Erianthes arundinaceus)*	Poaceae	Late monsoon to autumn	White, pale cream or reddish	A perennial grass
Shal (Sal)	*Shorea robusta*	Dipterocarpaceae	Spring	White or light yellow	Forest tree

Name	*Scientific name*	*Family*	*Flowering season*	*Flower colour*	*Remarks*
Shimul (Silk cotton tree)					
1. Lal (red)	*Bombax ceiba*	Bombacaceae	Spring	Red	Ornamental tree
2. Shwet (White)	*Ceiba pentandra*	Bombacaceae	Spring	White or rosy	Ornamental tree
3. Sonali (yellow)	*Cochlospermum religiosum*	Cochlospermaceae	Spring	Yellow	Ornamental tree
Shireesh (Siris)	*Albizia lebbek*	Mimosaceae	Spring, summer	Greenish white, yellow	Ornamental tree
Shephali (Night jasmine)	*Nyctanthes arbor-tristis*	Nyctanthaceae (Oleaceae)	Autumn to approach of winter (Hemanta)	White	Tall shrub, flowers nocturnal, scented
Shyaola (Algae)	1. *Chlamydomonas*	Chlamydomonadaceae			Non-flowering, chlorophyll-bearing thallophytes

Name	*Scientific name*	*Family*	*Flowering season*	*Flower colour*	*Remarks*
	2. *Volvox* sp.	Volvocaceae			
	3. *Spirogyra* sp.	Zygnemataceae			
Shwetmoni souravee (Sweet pea)	*Lathyrus odoratus*	Fabaceae	Winter	White, blue, maroon, violet, red and other colours	Light ornamental climber, flowers scented
Sojne (Drumstick)	*Moringa oleifera*	Moringaceae	Winter, spring	Yellowish white	Tree of medicinal value, flowers and fruit edible
Sorshe (Sarson)	1. *Brassica campestris var. sarson*	Brassicaceae	Spring	Yellow	Herbaceous oil seed producing crop
	2. *B. juncea*	Brassicaceae	Spring	Yellow	Herbaceous oil seed producing crop

Name	*Scientific name*	*Family*	*Flowering season*	*Flower colour*	*Remarks*
Seunti (Himalayan musk rose)	*Rosa brunonii*	Rosaceae	More or less in winter, spring and summer	White	Climbing rose, flowers scented
Sonajhuri (Australian wattle)	*Acacia auriculiformis*	Mimosaceae	Mostly in autumn but almost throughout the year	Yellow	Ornamental tree, scented flowers
Himjhuri (Indian cork tree)	*Millingtonia hortensis*	Bignoniaceae	Autumn, spring	Greenish white	Ornamental tree
Hena (Henna, Tree mignonette)	*Lawsonia inermis*	Lythraceae	Summer, monsoon	Light yellow, rose, red or white (according to variety)	Tall shrub

NUMERICAL FREQUENCY OF PLANTS OR FLOWERS IN LYRICS

Plant/Flower		*Frequency*
Ashath (Pipal)	..	5
Ashoka (Asoka tree)	..	22
Am (Mango)	..	21
Amlakee (Amla)	..	4
Amrha (Hog-plum)	..	1
Kachu (Arum)	..	1
Kadamba (Kadam)	..	28
Kanakchanpa (Maple twist)	..	3
Karabee (Oleander)	..	13
Kanchan (Mountain ebony)	..	3
Kaminee (Chinese box)	..	7
Kash (Thatch grass)	..	7
Kantalata (Thorny weeds)	..	1
Kunda (Kund-jasmine)	..	5
Kusum (Kusum)	..	46
Krishnakali (Four-O'-Clock plant)	..	3
Krishnachuda (Peacock flower)	..	2
Keya (Screwpine)	..	12
Golakchanpa (Pagoda tree)	..	1
Golap (Rose)	..	7
Chandan (Sandalwood tree)	..	11
Chameli (Spanish jasmine)	..	12
Chanpa (Golden champa)	..	25
Jaba (China rose)	..	3
Jam (Indian blackberry)	..	3
Jhau (Casuarina)	..	6
Jhumkolata (Passion flower)	..	2
Tamal (Egg tree)	..	18
Tal (Palmyra palm)	..	12
Doorba (Doob grass)	..	25

Plant/Flower		*Frequency*
Dolonchanpa (Ginger lily)	..	1
Dhan (Rice)	..	21
Dhutro (Thorn apple)	..	1
Nagkeshar (Iron wood tree)	..	1
Narikel (Coconut palm)	..	1
Neelshatadal (Blue lotus)	..	3
Padma (Lotus)	..	101
Palash (Parrot tree)	..	23
Parijat (Holy flower)	..	6
Parul (Trumpet flower)	..	8
Piyal (Cuddapah almond)	..	13
Bakul (Indian medlar)	..	73
Bot (Banyan tree)	..	6
Banaphul (Wild flowers)	..	9
Banamallika (Wild jasmine)	..	3
Banalata (Wild climber)	..	1
Bans (Bamboo)	..	30
Bela (Arabian jasmine)	..	7
Madhuk (Mohua tree)	..	1
Mallika (Malli jasmine)	..	18
Madhabee (Madhabi)	..	31
Malatee (Malti)	..	41
Joothee (Juin – jasmine)	..	28
Rangan (Ixora)	..	4
Rajaneegandha (Tuberose)	..	11
Labangalata (Luvunga)	..	1
Shamee (Sami)	..	2
Shara (Pin-reed grass)	..	3
Shal (Sal)	..	16
Shyaola (Algae)	..	3
Shephali (Night jasmine)	..	32
Shimul (Silk cotton tree)	..	1

Plant/Flower		*Frequency*
Shireesh (Siris)	..	11
Sojne (Drumstick)	..	1
Sarshe (Sarson)	..	2
Seunti (Himalayan Musk Rose)	..	2
Hena (Henna, Tree mignonette)	..	2

INDEX OF SONGS

List of songs in the text
(As appearing in Gitabitan)

Original Song	*Part of Gitabitan*
- Ajana khanir nootan manir	Prem
- Adhara madhuree dharechhi chhandobandhaney	”
- Ananter banee tumi	Prakriti
- Anek katha bolechhilem	Prem
- Anek diner shoonyata mor	Pooja
- Abelay jodi esechho amar boney	Prem O Prakriti
- Amalakamala sahaje jalera kole	Pooja
- Ashanti aj hanlo e kee	Prem Chitrangada
- Akash amay bhorlo aloy	Prakriti
- Akash taley daley daley	”
- Akash-bhara soorja-tara	”
- Akash hotey khasla tara	”
- Akashey aj kon charaner	Prem
- Akul keshey asey	”
- Achho akashpaney tuley matha	”
- Aj ki tahar barata pelo re	Prakriti
- Aj taray taray deepta shikhar	Bichitra
- Aj taler boner karatali	Prakriti
- Aj dakhina-batasey	”
- Aj dhaner kshetey roudra chhayay	”
- Aj pratham phuler pabo	”
- Aj bari jharey jhara jhara	”
- Aj shrabaner poornimatey	”
- Aj sabar rongey rong mishatey hobey	Prem

Original Song	*Part of Gitabitan*
- Aji ei gandha bidhura sameeraney	Prakriti
- Aji kamala mukula dal khulilo	”
- Aji kon dhan hotey bisvey amarey	Pooja
- Aji godhooli laganey ei badala gaganey	Prem
- Aji dakshina pabaney	Prem
- Aji dakhina duar khola	Prakriti
- Aji pallibalika alakaguchchha sajalo	”
- Aji barishana-mukharita	”
- Aji barsharater sheshey	”
- Aji sharata tapaney prabhata swapaney	Prakriti
- Aji hriday amar jay je bhesey	”
- Aju, sakhi, muhumuhu	Bhanusingher Padabalee
- Andhara ambarey prachanda dambaru	Prakriti
- Andhar shakha ujal kari	Natyageeti
- Adheka ghumey nayana chumey	Bichitra
- An go tora kar kee achhe	Prakriti
- Ananda tumi swami	Pooja
- Anmona anmona	Prem
- Abar esechhe ashadh akash chheye	Prakriti
- Amra khunji khelar sathi	Bichitra
- Amra chash kori anandey	”
- Amra jhore-pada phuladal	Prem O Prakriti
- Amra tarei jani tarei jani	Pooja
- Amra door akasher neshay matal	Natyageeti
- Amra nootan joubaneri doot	Bichitra
- Amra bendhechhi kasher guchchha	Prakriti
- Amra lakshmeechharhar dal	Bichitra
- Amader santiniketan	”
- Amader sakheere ke niye jabere	Natyageeti

Original Song	*Part of Gitabitan*
- Amar kantha hotey gan ke nila bhulaye	Prem
- Amar kee bedana seki jana	Prem O Prakriti
- Amar jeebana patra uchchhalia	Prem Shyama
- Amar dosar je jan ogo tarey ke janey	Prem
- Amar nayan tabo nayaner	"
- Amar nayana-bhulano eley	Prakriti
- Amar paran loye kee khela	Prem
- Amar praner parey choley gelo ke	"
- Amar praner majhe sudha achhe chao ki	"
- Amar mallika boney	Prakriti
- Amar matha nata korey	Pooja
- Amar malar phuler doley achhe lekha	Prakriti, Chandalika
- Amar rat pohalo sharad pratey	Prakriti
- Amar sakal kanta dhanya korey	Pooja
- Amar sonar Bangla	Swadesh
- Amarey karo tomar beena	Prem
- Amare dak dilo ke bhitarpaney	Bichitra
- Ami kan petey roi amar apan	Pooja
- Ami chai tanre	Chandalika
- Ami chahite esechhi shudhu ekkhani mala	Prem
- Ami chini go chini tomarey	"
- Ami takhan chhilem magana gahana	Prakriti,
- Ami to bujhechhi sab	Mayar khela
- Ami tomar sangey bendhechhi amar pran	Prem
- Ami pathbhola ek pathik esechhi	Prakriti
- Ami marer sagar padi debo	Pooja
- Ami shrabana akashey oi diyechhi pati	Prakriti Bichitra (Sanjojan)

Original Song	*Part of Gitabitan*
- Aye tora aye aye go	Prem O Prakriti
- Aye sakhee, ei bela (Neharo lo sahacharee)	Kalmrigaya
- Aye re mora phasal kati	Anushthanik
- Aro kichhukhan na hoy bosio pashey,	Prem
- Alo amar, alo ogo,	Bichitra
- Alor amala kamalakhani	Prakriti
- Ashadh kotha hotey aj peli chhada	"
- Ashadh sandhya ghaniye elo,	"
- Asa-jaoar pather dharey	Prem
- Aha, jagi pohalo bibhabaree	"
- Aha, tomar sangey praner khela	"
- Ahwan asila mahotsabey	Prakriti
- Utal-dhara badal jharey,	"
- Eki swapno ! eki maya !	Mayar khela
- Ekee e, e kee e, sthir chapala	Balmeeki Pratibha
- E ki karuna, karunamoya !	Pooja
- E pathe ami je gechhi bar bar	Prem
- Ei (e) abaran kshoy habey go	Pooja
- Ei kathatai chhilem bhuley	Prakriti
- Ei kathati mone rekho	Prem
- Ei to tomar alokdhenu	Pooja
- Ei to bhara holo phuley phuley	Natyageeti
- Ei to bhalo legechhilo	Bichitra
- Ei malin bastra chhadte hobey	Pooja
- Ei je heri go debi amari	Balmeeki Prativa
- Ei shrabon-bela badal-jhara	Prakriti
- Ei shrabaner buker bhitar	"
- Ei sakalbelar badal –andharey	"

Original Song	*Part of Gitabitan*
- Ei (ek) phaguner gan se amar	"
- Ektuku chhoan lagey	"
- Ekada, tumi priye,	Prem
- Ekla bosey eke eke anyamone	"
- Ekla bosey badal-sheshey shuni kato kee	Prakriti
- Ekla bosey, hero, tomar chhabi	Prem
- Ekhano tarey chokhe dekhini	"
- Eto din je bosechhilem path cheye	Prakriti
- Enechho oi shireesh bakul amer mukul	"
- Ebar abagunthana kholo	"
- Ebar amay dakley doorey	Pooja
- Ebar bidaybelar sur dharo dharo	Prakriti
- Ebar milan-haoaye haoaye	Prem
- Ebar rongiye gelo hriday gagan	Pooja
- Emni korey ghuriba doorey bahirey	"
- Elem natun deshey	Prem
- Eso' eso' basanta dharataley	Prakriti Chitrangadha
- Eso tharotharo kampita (eso eso basanta dharataley)	Mayar khela
- Esechhile tabu aso nai	Prakriti
- Eso eso ogo shyamachhayaghana din	Prem O Prakriti
- Eso eso praner utsabey	Anushthanik
- Eso go, jwele diye jao	Prakriti
- Eso go nootan jeeban	Bichitra
- Eso neepaboney chhayabeethitaley	Prakriti
- Eso shyamalasundara	"
- Eso hey eso sajalaghana	"
- O amar dhyaneri dhan	Prem
- O chand, tomay dola debe ke	Prakriti

Original Song	*Part of Gitabitan*
- O dekhbi re bhai, ay re chhutey	Kalmrigaya
- O dekha diye je chaley gelo	Prem
- O manjaree, O manjaree	Prakriti
- Oi asey oi oti bhairaba harashey	”
- Oi janalar kachhe bosey achhe	Natyageeti
- (Oi) Bhanglo hasir bandh	Prakriti
- Oi mahamanab asey	Anusthanik sangeet
- Oi malateelata doley	Prakriti
- Oi-je jhaderamegher koley	”
- Okey bandhibi ke re	Prem
- Ogo amar chira-achena	”
- Ogo amar shrabanamegher	Prakriti
- Ogo kishor, aji tomar dwarey	Prem
- Ogo ke jay banshari bajaye	”
- Ogo jaler ranee	Prem O Prakriti
- Ogo tumi panchadashee	Prakriti
- Ogo dakhin haoa	”
- Ogo nadee, apan bege	Bichitra
- Ogo padoshini, shuni banapathey	Prem
- Ogo badhoo sundaree,	Prakriti
- Ogo shephalibonera monera	”
- Ogo shono ke bajay	Prem
- Ogo saontali chheley	Prakriti
- Ogo sundara, ekada kee janey	Pooja
- Ogo swapnaswarupinee	Prem
- Oder sathey melao jara	Pooja
- Orey amar hriday amar	Prem
- Orey ke re eman jagay tokey	Pooja
- Orey grihabasee, khol dwar khol	Prakriti

Original Song	*Part of Gitabitan*
- Orey chitrarekhadorey bandhilo ke	Prem
- Orey jhad nemey aye	Prakriti,, Chitrangada
- Orey bakul, parul, orey	Prakriti, Prem O Prakriti
- Orey sabdhani pathik, barek	Bichitra
- Oli bar bar phire jay	Prem Mayar khela
- Olo shephali, olo shephali	Prakriti
- Ohey sundara, mamo grihey	Prem
- Kakhan je basanta gelo,	”
- Kakhan badal chhoan legey	Prakriti
- Kathin dharabhoomi e (Nami nami Bharatee, tabo kamalacharaney)	Balmeeki Pratibha
- Kata katha tarey chhila bolitey	Prem
- Kadamberi kanan gheri	Prakriti
- Kamalaboner madhuparaji	Bichitra
- Kandar samay alpo orey	Prem
- Kanpichhey dehalata tharo tharo	Prakriti
- Kar milana chao birahee	Pooja
- Kar jeno ei moner bedan	Prakriti
- Kal sakaley uthba mora	Kalmrigaya
- Kahar galay parabi ganer	Prem
- Kichhu bolbo boley esechhilem	Prakriti
- Kee gabo ami, kee shunabo	Pooja
- Kee bedana mor jano se kee tumi	Prem O Prakriti
- Kusume kusume charan chinha	Prakriti
- Krishnakoli ami tarei boli	Bichitra
- Ke amare jeno enechhe dakia	Prem

Original Song	*Part of Gitabitan*
- Ke uthe daki	”
- Ke elo aji e ghor nisheethey	Kalmrigaya Balmeeki Pratibha
- Keno amay pagal korey jas	Prem
- Keno go apan-mone	Balmeeki Pratibha
- Keno pantha, e chanchalata	Prakriti
- Keno jaminee na-jetey jagaley na	Prem
- Keno re etai jabar twara	”
- Ko tunhu bolabi moy	Bhanusingher Padabalee
- Kotha hotey shunte jeno pai	Prem
- Kothao amar hariye jaoar	Natyageeti
- Kothay phiris param shesher anweshaney	Bichitra
- Kothay se ushamoyee pratima	Balmeeki Pratibha
- Kon khepa shraban chhutey elo	Prakriti
- Kon gahana aranye tarey	Prem
- Kon debata se kee parihasey	Prem Chitrangada
- Kon puratan praner taney	Prakriti
- Klanta banshir shesh raginee	Prem
- Klanta jakhan amrakolir kal	Prakriti
- Kshama karo more sakhee	Natyageeti
- Khela kar, khela kar tora	”
- Gahana kusuma kunja majhey	Bhanusingher Padabalee
- Gahana ghana boney piyal-tamal	Prem
-Gahana ratey shrabandhara porhichhe jhorey	Prakriti
- Ganguli mor shaibaleri dal	Prem

Original Song	*Part of Gitabitan*
- Ganer jharnatalay tumi	Pooja
- Ganer dali bhorey de go	Prem
-Ganer bhitar diye jakhan	Pooja
- Ganer surer asankhani	"
- Gopana kathati rabey na gopaney	Prem
- Golap phul phutiye achhe	Prem O Prakriti
- Gharete bhramar elo gunguniye	Prem
- Ghumer ghana gahan hotey	Prem Chandalika
- Chapala tabo nabeena ankhi duti	Prem
- Charanarekha taba je pathey diley lekhi	Prakriti, Prem O Prakriti
- Chal chal bhai twara korey mora	Kalmrigaya, Balmeeki Prativa
- Chaley chhalo chhalo nadeedhara	Prakriti
- Chaley jay mori hai basanter din	"
- Chander hasir bandh bhengechhe	Prem
- Chiradibas naba madhuree, naba shova	Pooja
- Chhaya ghanaichhe boney boney	Prakriti
- Chhi chhi sakha, kee koriley	Parishishta()
- Chhinna patar sajai taranee	Pooja
- Chhutir banshi bajlo je oi	Prem
- Jale-doba chikan shyamal	Prem O Prakriti
- Jagichhe poornima poorna neelamborey (E ki swapna! e eki maya!)	Mayar khela
- Jani go, din jabe	Pooja
- Jani jani esechho e pathey moner bhuley	Prem O Prakriti

Original Song	*Part of Gitabitan*
- Jani jani, tumi esechho e pathey	Prem
- Jani, jani holo jabar ayojan	Prem
- Jeebaneye ki pratham basanta elo, elo	Prem O Prakriti
- Jham jham ghana ghana	Kalmrigaya
- Jhankda chuler meyer katha	Prem O Prakriti
- Taper taper bandhan katuk	Prakriti
- Tabey tai hok (sangeet katha)	Chitrangada
- Taree amar hathat dubey jay	Bichitra
- Tarun prater arun akash	Prem O Prakriti
- Tarutaley chhinnabrinta malateer phul	Natyageeti
- Timira-abagunthaney badana taba dhaki	Prakriti
- Tui ayre, kachhey aya, (O bhai, dekhey ja kato phul tulechhi)	Kalmrigaya
- Tumi amaye dekechhiley	Prem
- Tumi ushara sonara bindu	Bichitra
- Tumi ke go, sakheere keno	Mayar khela
- Tumi kon kananer phul	Prem
- Tumi to sei jabei choley	Prem O Prakriti
- Tumi je cheye achho akash bhorey	Pooja
- Tumi dhanya dhanya hey, dhanya tabo prem	"
- Tumi je surer agun lagiye diley	"
- Trishnar shanti, sundar kanti	Prakriti, Chitrangada
- Tomra hasia bahia chalia jao	Bichitra
- Tomader dan jasher dalay	"
- Tomay sajabo jataney	Natyageeti

Original Song	*Part of Gitabitan*
- Tomar asan patbo kothay	Prakriti
- Tomar kati-tater dhati	Natyageeti
- Tomar kachhe e bar magi	Pooja
- Tomara geeti jagalo smriti	Prem
- Tomar gopan kathati sakhee	Prem
- Tomar nam janiney, sur jani	Prakriti
- Tomar bas kotha je, pathik ogo	Prakriti
- Tomar beena amar monomajhey	Pooja
- Tomar moner ekti katha amay balo	Prem
- Tomar mohanaroope ke roy bhuley	Prakriti
- Tomar sonar thalay sajabo aj	Pooja
- Tomari namey nayan melinu	"
- Doi chai go, doi chai	Chandalika
- Dakhin haoa, jago jago	Prakriti
- Dinasheshey basanta ja praney gelo boley	"
- Dinashesher ranga mukul	Prem
- Deep nibey gechhe mamo nisheethasameere	"
- Duksha je tor noyrey chirantan	Pooja
- Durasha jagay (Mora jaley sthaley kato chhaley	Mayar khela
- Doordeshee sei rakhal chheley	Bichitra
- Doorer bandhu surer dooteerey	Prem
- Delo, sakhi, de paraiye galey	Mayar khela
- Deoa neoa phiriye deoa	Pooja
- Dekho, shuktara ankhi meli chay	Prakriti
- Doley, premer dolan chanpa	"
- Doshee karo amay, doshee karo	Chandalika
-Dharanee, doorey cheye keno aj achhis jegey	Prakriti
- Dharaneer gaganer milaner chhandey	"

Original Song	*Part of Gitabitan*
- Dhara se je dey nai	Prem, Shyama
- Dhoosar jeebaner godhoolitey	Prem
- Naba-kunda-dhabaladala-susheetala	Prakriti
- Naba basanter daner dali	Prakriti, Chandalika
- Nami, nami charaney	Pooja
- Nami, nami, Bharatee, taba kamala charaney	Balmeeki Pratibha
- Namo namo shacheechitaranjana	Natyageeti
- Na chahile jare paoa jay	Prem
- Na, jeyo na, jeyo na ko,	Prakriti
- Nai jodi ba ele tumi	Prem
- Nach, Shyama, taley taley	Natyageeti
- Nachiba, sakhee, (Ay lo sajanee, sabey miley)	Kalmrigaya
- Nitya tomar je phul photey	Pooja
- Nidrahara rater e gan	Prem
- Nibid ama-timira hotey	Prakriti
- Nirjan ratey nihshabda charan patey	Prem O Prakriti
- Nishar swapan chhutla re	Pooja
- Neel anjanghana punjachhayay	Prakriti
- Neel akasher koney koney	"
- Neel digantey oi phuler agun	"
- Neel nabaghaney ashadh gaganey	"
- Neelanjanachhaya, prafulla kadambabon	Prem
- Noopura beje jaye rinirini	"
- Nrityera taley taley, nataraj	Bichitra
- Neharo lo sahacharee	Kalmrigaya
- Pathik paran, chal, chal se pathey tui	Prem

Original Song	*Part of Gitabitan*
- Pakhee baley, chanpa, amarey kao	Bichitra
- Padaprantey rakho sebakey	Pooja
- Panthapakheer rikta kulaye	Prem
- Purano janiya cheyo na amarey	"
- Purano sei diner katha	Prem O Prakriti
- Puree hotey paliyechhe je purasundaree	Shyama
- Poorna holo basna (Nami nami, Bharatee, taba kamala-charaney)	Balmeeki Prativa
- Peyechhi sandhan tabo antarjamee	Pooja
- Pohalo pohalo bibhaboree	Prakriti
- Poush toder dak diyechhe	"
- Pratidin taba gatha	Pooja
- Prabhate bimala anandey	"
- Prabhu, elem kothay	Pooja O Prarthana
- Prahar shesher aloy ranga	Natyageeti
- Prangane mor shireesh shakhay phagunmasey	Bichitra
- Pran niye to satkechhirey	Kalmrigaya, Balmeeki Pratibha
- Premey praney ganey gandhey	Pooja
- Phagun-haoay rongey rongey	Prakriti
- Phagun, haoay haoay korechhi je dan	"
- Phagunera nabeena anandey	"
- Phagunera poornima elo kar lipi hatey	"
- Phirbey na ta jani	Prem
- Bakulgandhey banya elo	Prakriti
- Bajaorey mohanbanshi	Bhanusingher Padabalee

Original Song	*Part of Gitabitan*
- Bondhu, tomay korbo raja	Prem
- Bondhua, hiya-'por aorey	Bhanusingher Padabalee
- Bal, golap, morey bal	Prem
- Boli, O amar golapbala	Prem O Prakriti
- Balo sakhee, balo tari nam	Prem
- Baki ami rakhbo na	Prakriti
- Banchan banchi, maren mori	Pooja
- Bajao amare bajao	"
- Bajila, kahara beena madhur swarey	Prem
- Baje karuna surey	"
- Baje baje ramyabeena baje	Pooja
- Bajo re banshori, bajo	Natyageeti
- Badaladiner prathama kadamphul	Prakriti
- Badal-dhara holo sara	"
- Badal baul bajay re ektara	"
- Barey barey phirey phire tomar paney	Prem O Prakriti
- Banshori bajatey chahi,	Prem
- Bahir holem ami apan	Natyageeti
- Biday korechho jarey nayanajaley	prem Mayar khela
- Biday niye giyechhilem barey barey	Prakriti
- Biday jakhan chaibey tumi	"
- Bujhi elo, bujhi elo orey pran	Prem O Prakriti
- Brishtishesher haoa kiser khonje	Prakriti
- Byakul bakuler phuley	"
- Bhara thak smritisudhay	Prem

Original Song	*Part of Gitabitan*
- Bhalobese, sakhee, nibhritey jataney	"
- Bhor thekey aj badal chhutechhe	Prakriti
- Bhor holo jei shrabanasharbaree	Prakriti
- Madhu-gandhe-bhara mridu snigdhachhaya	Prakriti
- Madhura basanta esechhe Mayar khela	Prakriti,
- Madhura madhura dhwani bajey	Bichitra
- Madhur milan	Natyageeti
- Madhyadiney jabe gan bandha karey pakhi	Prakriti
- Madhyadiner bijan batayane	"
- Mono mor meghera sangee	Prakriti
- Mon je baley chini chini	"
- Mone kee dwidha rekhey geley chaley	Prem
- Mone holo periye elem aseem path	Prem O Prakriti
- Mone holo, jeno periye elem	Prakriti
- Manomandira sundaree!	Natyageeti
- Manomohana, gahana jamineesheshey	Pooja
- Mama joubana nikunje gahe pakhee	Prem
- Marana re, tunhun mama shyam saman	"
- Mari lo kar banshi	Prakriti
- Madhabee hathat kotha hotey	"
- Man-abhiman bhasiye diye	Prem
- Milan rati pohalo, bati	"
- Mukhapane cheye dekhi, bhay hay mone	"
- Megha-chhaye sajala baye mon amar	"
- Megher koley rod hesechhe	Prakriti
- Mor beena othey	"

Original Song	*Part of Gitabitan*
- Mor bhabonarey kee haoay matalo	”
- Mor maraney tomar hobey joy	Pooja
- Mor sandhay tumi sundar beshey esechha	”
- Mora bhangba tapas	Prakriti
- Jakhan padbey na mor payer chinnha	Bichitra
- Jatokhan tumi amay bosiye rakho	Pooja
- Jadi holo jabar kshan	Prem
- Jaboi ami jaboi ogo,	Bichitra
- Jay din, shrabanadin jay	Prakriti
- Je kebol paliye bedaye	Bichitra
- Je din phutlo kamal	Pooja
- Jeo na, jeo na phirey	Prem, Mayar khela
- Jaubanasaraseeneere milana shatadala	Prem
- Rajanee pohailo, chalechhe jatreedal	Pooja O Prarthana
- Rajaneer shesh tara	Pooja
- Rabir kiraney phutia (Bhalobesey dukh seo sukh)	Mayar Khela
- Rakho rakho re jeebaney jeebanballabhey	Pooja
- Rangapadapadmajuge pranami go bhabadara!	Balmeeki Pratibha
- Rodan-bhara e basanta	Prem, Chitrangada
- Lakshmee jakhan asbe takhan	Pooja
- Laho laho, phirey laho	Chitrangada
- Likhan tomar dhulay hoyechhe dhuli,	Prem
- Boney jadi phutlo kusum	”
- Barshanamandrito andhakarey	”
- Basanta aolo re!	Bhanusingher Padabalee

Original Song	*Part of Gitabitan*
- Basanta-prabhatey ek malateer phul	Natyageeti
- Basanta se jay to hesey	Prem
- Basantee, hey bhubanamohinee	Prakriti
- Bidhi dagar ankhi jodi diyechhiley	Prem O Prakriti
- Bishwabeenarabey bishwajanamohichhe	Prakriti
- Bedona kee bhashay re	"
- Bela jay bahia	Chitrangada
- Baishakher ei bhorer haoa	Prakriti
- Sharat tomar arun alor anjalee	"
- Sharat alor kamalaboney	"
- Shanwana gaganey ghora ghanaghata	"
- Shiuli phul, shiuli phul	"
- Shiuli-phota phurolo jei	Prakriti
- Sheeter boney kon se kathin asbey boley	"
- Sheeter haoar laglo nachan	"
- Shudhu ekti gandoosh jal	Chandalika
- Shuno nalinee, kholo go ankhi	Prem O Prakriti
- Shuno lo shuno lo balika	Bhanusingher Padabalee
- Shuni oi runujhunu	Natyageeti
- Shubhra naba shankha taba gagan bhari bajey	Pooja
- Shesh ganeri resh niye jao choley	Prakriti
- Shyam, mukhe taba madhur adharmey	Bhanusingher Padabalee
- Shyam re, nipata kathin	"
- Shraban, tumi batasey kar abhas peley	Prakriti
- Shrabanbarishana par hoye	"
- Shrabanera pabaney akul bishanna sandhay	Prem

Original Song	Part of Gitabitan
- Shrabaner baridhara	Prem O Prakriti
- Sakaruna benu bajaye ke jay	Prem
- Sakali phuralo swapana-prai	Kalmrigaya
- Sakalbelar aloy bajey	Prem
- Sakhee, kee dekha dekhiley tumi (Sangeetkatha)	Chitrangada
- Sakhee, pratidin hay esey phirey jay ke	Prem
- Saghana gahano ratri	Prakriti
- Sajani sajani Radhika lo	Bhanusingher Padabalee
- Satimira rajanee, sachakita sajanee	"
- Sabar sathey chaltechhilo	Prem
- Sahasa dalpala tor utala je	Prakriti
- Sajabo tomarey hey phul diye diye	Prem
- Sara jeeban dilo alo	Pooja
- Sara nishi chhilem shueye bijan bhunye	Prakriti
- Sarthaka karo sadhana,	Pooja
- Sukhey achhi, sukhey achhi	Prem, Mayar khela
- Suneel sagarer shyamal kinarey	Prem
- Sundara hridiranjana tumi	"
- Surer guru, dao go surer deeksha	Pooja
- Se asey dheerey	Prem
- Se kon boner harin chhilo amar mone	Bichitra
- Se din amay bolechhiley	Prakriti
- Sei to tomar pather bondhu	"
- Sei bhalo, sei bhalo	Prem
- Swarnabarney samujjal naba champadaley	Chandalika
- Hater dhula soyna je ar	Bichitra

Original Song	*Part of Gitabitan*
- Hai re, orey jay na ki jana	Prem
- Hai hemantalakshmee, tomar	Prakriti
- Har-mana har	Pooja
- Hasi keno nai O nayaney	Prem O Prakriti
- Himsay unmatta prithvee	Pooja
- Himerarater oi gaganer deepgulirey	Prakriti
- Hriday amar nacherey ajike	"
- Hridayaka sadh mishaola hridaye	Bhanusingher Padabalee
- Hridaye chhiley jegey	Prakriti
- Hridaye mandrila damaru guruguru	"
- Hridaye rakho go, debee, charan tomar	Natyageeti
- Hey kshaniker atithi	Prem
- Hey nirupama	"
- Hey madhabee, dwidha keno	Prakriti
- Hey sakha, barata peyechhi	Prem
- Hey sannyasee, himgiri phele	Prakriti
- Hemantey kon basanteri banee	"
- Heri tabo bimalamukhabhati	Pooja
- Hyadey go nandaranee	Bichitra

INDEX OF ENGLISH NAMES

English Name	*Name as in text*	*Page Number*
Acacia (Thorny)	Kanta negeshwar	179
Algae	Shyaola, Shaibal	161
Amla	Amlokee, Amloki	10
Arabian jasmine	Bela, Beli, Bel, Ballika	70
Argyreia	Banaphul	130
Arum	Kachu	13
Asoka	Ashok, Banjul	3
Australian wattle	Sonajhuri, Akashmoni	177
Bamboo	Bans, Benu	133
Banyan tree	Bot	127
Barbados pride	Krishnachuda	37
Barleria	Janti	61, 179
Bermuda grass	Doorba	88
Bird's eye bush	Basantee, Ramdhanchanpa	175
Blue dawn flower	Banalata	130

N.B. For botanical names vide Table on 'Flowering Calendar'.

English Name	*Name as in text*	*Page Number*
Blue lotus	Neelshatadal, Neelpadma, Neelambuj	102
'Bo'-tree	Ashath, Ashathwa, Ashwath	1
Bougainvillea	Baganbilas	178
Butterfly lily	Dolonchanpa	92
Casuarina	Jhau	78
China rose	Jaba	53
Chinese box	Kaminee	25
Clematis	Tarajhara	171
Clerodendron	Ghentu, Bhanti, Banaphul	130
Cockspur coral tree	Parijat	113
Coconut tree	Narikel	100
Cuddapah almond	Piyal	118
Cypress vine	Tarulata, Banalata	130
Doob grass	Doorba	88
Drumstick	Sojney	163
Egg tree	Tamal, Tamalee	82
Egyptian privet	Hena	169

English Name	*Name as in text*	*Page Number*
Emblic myrobalan	Amlokee, Amloki	10
Fallen stars	Tarajhara	171
Flamboyant	Gulmohar	39
Flame of fire	Agnishikha, Langul	171
Flame of the forest	Palash, Kimshuk	110
Four O' Clock plant	Krishnakali, Sandhyaphul, Sandhyamalatee, Sandhyakali	35
Frywood tree	Shireesh	154
Ginger lily	Dolonchanpa	92
Glory lily	Agnishikha, langul	171
Gol mohr	Gulmohar	37
Golden champa	Chanpa, Champak, Champa	49
Golden shower	Sonajhuri, Akashmoni	177
Henna	Hena	169
Himalayan musk rose	Seunti, Sevantee	167
Hog-plum	Amrha	12
Holy tree	Parijat, Mandar, Paltemadar	113

English Name	*Name as in text*	*Page Number*
Honey wreath	Madhumanjaree, Madhumalatee Haragouree	175
Indian blackberry	Jam, Jambu	55
Indian butter tree	Madhuk, Mahua	136
Indian cork tree	Himjhuri, Akashnim	178
Indian medlar	Bakul	121
Iron-wood tree	Nagkeshar	98
Ixora	Rangan	141
Jasmines	Jnui jateeya phul	64
Java plum	Jam, Jambu	55
Jnui-jasmine	Joothee, Junthi, Juin	64
Kadam	Kadamba, Kadam, Neepa	14
Kund-jasmine	Kunda	59
Lac tree	Kusum (I)	31
Lantana	Banaphul	130
Lotus	Padma, Shatadal, Nalinee, Kamal	104
Luvunga	Labangalata	145

English Name	*Name as in text*	*Page Number*
Madagascar periwinkle	Tarajhara, Nayantara	171
Madhabi	Madhabee, Madhabika	138
Mahua tree	Madhuk, Mohua	136
Malli-jasmine	Mallika, Malli	72
Malti (Jasmine and others)	i) Malatee (Juin) ii) Malateelata (Aganosma)	74 74
Mango	Am, Amra, Amua, Sahakar	7
Maple twist	Kanakchanpa	18
Mimosa (thorny)	Shiakanta, Kantalata	29
Morning glory	Peyalee, Banaphul, Banalata	130,173
Mountain ebony	Kanchan	22
Narcissus	Nargis, Nargesh	180
Night jasmine	Shephali, Shiuli, Shephalika, Parijat	157
Oleander	Karabee	20
Oncoba	Oncoba, Ispani	180
Orange jessamine	Kaminee	25
Pagoda tree	Golakchanpa	42

English Name	*Name as in text*	*Page Number*
Palmyra palm	Tal, Talee	85
Parrot tree	Palash, Kimshuk	110
Passion flower	Jhumkolata	80
Peacock flower	Krishnachuda, Radhachuda	37
Philippine violet	Janti	179
Pipal	Ashath, Ashathwa, Ashwath	1
Pin-reed grass	Shara	148
Prickly amaranth	Kantanotey, Kantalata	29
Purple wreath	Neelmonilata	172
Railway creeper	Banalata	130
Rangoon creeper	Madhumalatee, Madhumanjaree	175
Rice plant	Dhan, Aush	93
Rose	Golap	44
Rose bay	Karabee	20
Rose of Venezuela	Parijat	113
Ruellia (wild)	Banaphul	130
Safflower	Kusum (II)	31
Sal	Shal, Ashwakarna	149

English Name	*Name as in text*	*Page Number*
Sami	Shamee	147
Sandalwood tree	Chandan	47
Sarson	Sorshey	165
Screwpine	Keya, Ketakee	39
Sensitive plant	Lajjabati, Banaphul	130
She-oak	Jhau	74
Silk cotton tree (red, white, yellow)	Shimul (lal, shwet, sonali)	152
Siris	Shireesh	154
Siuli	Shephali, Shieuli, Shephalika, Parijat	113, 157
Spanish cherry	Bokul	121
Spanish jasmine	Chameli, Jati	61
Sweet pea	Shwetmoni souravee	177
Thatch grass	Kash	27
Thorn apple	Dhutro	96
Thorny weeds	Kantalata	29
Tree mignonette	Hena	169

English Name	*Name as in text*	*Page Number*
Trumpet flower	Parul	116
Tuberose	Rajaneegandha	143
White paveta	Banpulak, Banaphul	174
White poinsettia	Phuljhuri	179
Wild flowers	Banaphul	130
Wild climbers	Banalata	130
Wild jasmine	Banmallika	68
Woman's tongue tree	Shireesh	154
Yellow-berried night shade	Kantikari, Kantalata	29

LIST OF COLOUR PHOTOGRAPHS

Plants/Flowers

Pipal (Ashath), Asoka tree (Ashok), Mango tree (Am), Mango floral bunch, Amla (Amlokee), Hog plum (Amrha), Arum (Kachu)

(Photograph Nos. 1-6)

Kadam tree, Kadam flowers, Maple twist tree (Kanakchanpa), Maple twist flower, Oleander (Karabee) – red, white, rose, Mountain ebony (Kanchan) – red, dev, white, Chinese box (Kaminee), Thatch grass (Kash)

(Photograph Nos. 7-12)

Thorny weeds (Kantalata) – Kusum tree (1), flowers (1), Safflower (Kusum, 2), Four O' Clock plant (Krishnakali) – white and red flowers, Peacock flower (Krishnachuda), Screwpine plant (Keya), Screwpine flower

(Photograph Nos. 13-17)

Pagoda tree (Golakchanpa) – red, white, Golap (Rose), Sandalwood tree (Chandan), Golden champa, Champa flower, China rose (Jaba), Indian black berrytree (Jam)

(Photograph Nos. 18-23)

Jasmine: Kund (scented), Kund (Kunda), Spanish jasmine (Jati/chameli) – Juin – jasmine (Joothee), Wild jasmine (Banmallika), Arabian jasmine (Bela)

(Photograph Nos. 24-29)

Malli-jasmine (Mallika), Malti (Malatee-jasmine), Casuarina (Jhau), Passion flower (Jhumkolata), Egg-tree (1, 2) (Tamal)

(Photograph Nos. 30-34)

Bengali names in parenthesis. For botanical names vide 'Flowering Calendar'.

Plants/Flowers

Palmyra palm (Tal), Doob grass (Doorba), Ginger lily (Dolonchanpa), Rice plant (Dhan), Thorn apple (Dhutro), Iron-wood tree (Nagkeshar) – tree, flowers,
(Photograph Nos. 35-40)

Nirikel (Coconut tree), Blue lotus (Neelshatadal): Lotus (Padma) – i) red, ii) white, Parrot tree (Palash), Holy tree (Parijat) Parul (trumpet tree)
(Photograph Nos. 41-46)

Cuddapah almond (Piyal) – tree and flowers, Indian medlar (Bokul) – tree, flowers and fruits, Banyan tree (Bot) – massive tree canopy, props, fruits, Wild climbers (Banalata), Wild flowers (Banaphul), Bamboo (Bans, Benu)
(Photograph Nos. 47-51)

Mohua tree (Madhuk), Madhabi (Madhabee) Ixora (Rangan), Tuberose (Rajaneegandha),Luvunga (Labangalata), Sami (Samee)
(Photograph Nos. 52-57 (a))

Sami (Shamee) – 1, 2, Pin-reed grass (Shara), Sal (Shal), Silk cotton tree (Shimul), Siris (Shireesh), Night jasmine (Shephali).
(Photograph Nos. 57(b)-62)

Algae (Shyaola), Drumstick (Sojney), Sarson (Sorshey), Himalayan musk rose (Seunti), Tree mignonette (Hena).
(Photograph Nos. 63-65)

PLANTS AND FLOWERS NAMED BY TAGORE

Plants/Flowers

1) Glory lily (Agnishikha), 2) Madagascar periwinkle (Tarajhara 1), *Clematis* (Tarajhara 2), 3) Purple wreath (Neelmonilata), 4) Morning glory (Peyalee)

(Photograph Nos. 1-4)

5) White paveta (Banpulak), 6) Bird's eye bush (Basantee), 7) Rangoon creeper Honey Wreath (Madhumanjaree), 8) Sweet pea (Shwetmoni souravee), Australian wattle Golden Shower (Sonajhuri), Indian cork tree (Himjhuri)

(Photograph Nos. 5-10)

Bougainvillea (Baganbilas), White poinsettia (Phuljuri), Philippine violet (Jati) – i) purple flowers, ii) white flowers, Acacia sp. (Kanta nageshwar), Narcissus (Nargesh), Oncoba (Ispani).

(Photograph Nos. 11-16)